The Latest UK Air Fryer Cookbook 2023

1600 *Days Super-Easy, Crispy and Tasty Air Fryer Recipes, Enjoy Freshly-Cooked Mains and Sides with 100% Taste for Busy Weeknight Meals*

Tonja R. Sea

CONTENTS

Fish & Seafood Recipes 42

Vegetarian & Vegan Recipes 50

INTRODUCTION

Nowadays, Air Fryer is more and more popular, but many people can't make the best use of it. They don't know what food the Air Fryer can make. This is also the original intention of Tonja R. Sea to write this cookbook. With rich cooking experience, Tonja R. Sea compiled this cookbook of Air Fryer, perfectly blending the convenience of Air Fryer with health-conscious dining. This cookbook is your ultimate guide to exploring the countless possibilities that your Air Fryer has to offer while sticking to a diet that enhances wellness and vitality.

This cookbook is designed for anyone who wants to enjoy the crispy, crunchy textures of their favorite fried foods without compromising their health goals. Whether you're new to the world of Air Fryer or a seasoned pro looking to expand your culinary repertoire, this book offers a wealth of recipes that require less oil but deliver all the flavor.

The "Air Fryer Diet Cookbook" boasts an assortment of recipes that span meals of the day and a myriad of cuisines. From mouthwatering breakfast options to hearty dinners, and from local favorites to international delicacies, each dish is thoughtfully crafted to provide nutritious, balanced meals without sacrificing taste or satisfaction.

Every recipe in this book comes with easy-to-follow instructions, an accessible list of ingredients, and nutritional information, ensuring you have everything you need to stay on track with your diet. Moreover, the recipes cater to a variety of dietary preferences, including vegetarian, vegan, gluten-free, and low-carb options.

Alongside the recipes, you'll find practical tips and tricks on how to get the most out of your Air Fryer, as well as insights into the science behind air frying and its health benefits. You'll also discover how to adapt traditional frying recipes for the Air Fryer, enabling you to enjoy healthier versions of your beloved fried foods.

With the "Air Fryer Diet Cookbook," you're not just getting a collection of recipes - you're embarking on a journey of culinary discovery and transformation that will inspire you to experiment, indulge, and celebrate healthy food in a whole new way. Dive into the flavorsome world of air frying and enjoy the journey towards a healthier, more balanced lifestyle!

Is Air Fryer healthier?

Compared to traditional cooking methods, Air Fryers offer a healthier alternative to traditional frying methods by significantly reducing the amount of oil used in the cooking process.

Lower Fat Content: Traditional deep frying submerges food in oil, which increases the fat content of the final product. Air Fryers, on the other hand, circulate hot air to cook food, which typically requires less than a tablespoon of oil. This results in food that has less fat but can still achieve a similar taste and texture to deep-fried food.

Fewer Calories: Less oil means fewer calories. So if you're watching your caloric intake, an Air Fryer can be a great tool to use.

Reduced Acrylamide Formation: Fried food can lead to the formation of acrylamide, a potentially harmful substance that forms in some foods during high-heat cooking methods like frying. Studies have shown that using an Air Fryer can reduce acrylamide content by 90% compared to deep frying.

Versatility: Air Fryers aren't just for fried food. They can also roast, bake, and grill a variety of foods, making it easier to prepare healthier meals.

However, keep in mind that while using an Air Fryer can be healthier than deep frying, it does not necessarily make unhealthy food healthy. The nutritional value of the food also depends on the ingredients you use. For example, air frying a breaded, processed chicken nugget may be lower in fat than deep frying it, but it's still not as healthy as a piece of grilled chicken breast.

What kind of ingredients do you choose for your Air Fryer?

Choosing the right ingredients for your Air Fryer can make a big difference in the final results.

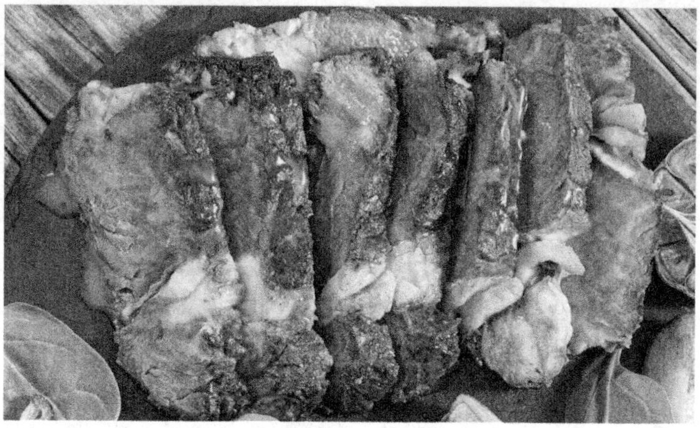

1.High-Quality Proteins

Lean meats and fish often turn out great in an Air Fryer. Go for chicken, turkey, lean cuts of pork, salmon, or white fish. Tofu can also be a good choice for vegetarians and vegans.

2.Healthy Oils

Since air frying requires less oil than traditional frying, opt for healthier oils when necessary. Olive oil, avocado oil, or canola oil are good options. Remember to use oil sparingly, a light spray is often enough.

3.Fresh or Frozen Vegetables

Most vegetables air fry beautifully, achieving a crispy texture on the outside while staying tender on the inside. Options include but are not limited to potatoes, carrots, broccoli, Brussels sprouts, bell peppers, and zucchini. Frozen veggies can also work, but you may need to adjust the cooking time.

4.Breadings and Coatings

If you're trying to replicate the texture of deep-fried foods, you'll want to use some form of breading. Panko breadcrumbs, crushed cornflakes, or almond flour for a low-carb option can all work well. You can also use a light batter, but be cautious as it can drip and make a mess.

5.Spices and Herbs

Don't forget to season your food. Fresh or dried herbs, spices, rubs, or marinades can all be used to add flavor to your dishes.

6.Prepackaged Foods

Many prepackaged foods, like frozen fries, spring rolls, or breaded fish, can be cooked in the Air Fryer. They're usually quicker and turn out crispier than when baked in the oven.

Remember that Air Fryers work by circulating hot air, so you want to avoid lightweight ingredients that might get blown around. Also, very wet or loose batters can drip and create smoke. It's important to avoid overfilling the basket, as overcrowding can lead to uneven cooking.

Common questions related to Air Fryer

- **What containers can I put in my Air Fryer?**

Baking bowls, baking trays, special paper cups; paper for fryers; tinfoil type; moulds.

- **How to use greaseproof paper or tinfoil?**

Use tinfoil for vegetables and meat, and greaseproof paper for pastry baking.

Note: 1. When using baking paper, be sure to put enough food to hold the paper down, otherwise the paper will be blown up and touch the heating tube and there will be a risk of fire.

2. The height of the paper should be half the height of the fryer.

3. If the food is solid, it is not recommended to use all types of paper as it will increase the cooking time and the build-up of grease will affect the taste.

- **When do I need to preheat?**

Preheat pastry and bread and thick meat.

Pre-heating precautions: Pre-heating must be done on an empty burner. Preheat once on the day of use.

- **How do I decide whether to lay my food flat or on top of each other?**

Semi-finished products and meats can be stored flat. Fruits and vegetables can be stacked

Tips:Meat can easily be heated unevenly if stacked, so it is best to leave a gap when laying it out.

- **Which ingredients need to be brushed with oil?**

Vegetables and seafood can be brushed with oil in moderation for better taste.

- **How can I tell when to turn the food?**

For meat: turn once halfway through; for vegetables: turn two to three times.

- **How do I clean my Air Fryer?**

For everyday cleaning, scrub the bottom and sides with a damp paper towel, and use detergent and water to clean the fryer, but do not use sharp objects such as wire balls to avoid damaging the fryer's coating and reducing the life of the Air Fryer.

If you have a lot of grease, you can use baking soda or white vinegar, mix with hot water and then bake the Air Fryer at 180 degrees for 10 minutes, then clean with detergent.

Take this Air Fryer recipe book on a culinary journey, with a wealth of nutritious recipes, from breakfast and dinner to snacks, so that you can enjoy your life with three meals a day!

Measurement Conversions

BASIC KITCHEN CONVERSIONS & EQUIVALENTS

DRY MEASUREMENTS CONVERSION CHART

3 TEASPOONS = 1 TABLESPOON = 1/16 CUP

6 TEASPOONS = 2 TABLESPOONS = 1/8 CUP

12 TEASPOONS = 4 TABLESPOONS = 1/4 CUP

24 TEASPOONS = 8 TABLESPOONS = 1/2 CUP

36 TEASPOONS = 12 TABLESPOONS = 3/4 CUP

48 TEASPOONS = 16 TABLESPOONS = 1 CUP

METRIC TO US COOKING CONVERSIONS

OVEN TEMPERATURES

120 °C = 250 °F

160 °C = 320 °F

180° C = 350 °F

205 °C = 400 °F

220 °C = 425 °F

LIQUID MEASUREMENTS CONVERSION CHART

8 FLUID OUNCES = 1 CUP = 1/2 PINT = 1/4 QUART

16 FLUID OUNCES = 2 CUPS = 1 PINT = 1/2 QUART

32 FLUID OUNCES = 4 CUPS = 2 PINTS = 1 QUART

= 1/4 GALLON

128 FLUID OUNCES = 16 CUPS = 8 PINTS = 4 QUARTS = 1 GALLON

BAKING IN GRAMS

1 CUP FLOUR = 140 GRAMS

1 CUP SUGAR = 150 GRAMS

1 CUP POWDERED SUGAR = 160 GRAMS

1 CUP HEAVY CREAM = 235 GRAMS

VOLUME

1 MILLILITER = 1/5 TEASPOON

5 ML = 1 TEASPOON

15 ML = 1 TABLESPOON

240 ML = 1 CUP OR 8 FLUID OUNCES

1 LITER = 34 FL. OUNCES

WEIGHT

1 GRAM = .035 OUNCES

100 GRAMS = 3.5 OUNCES

500 GRAMS = 1.1 POUNDS

1 KILOGRAM = 35 OUNCES

US TO METRIC COOKING CONVERSIONS

1/5 TSP = 1 ML

1 TSP = 5 ML

1 TBSP = 15 ML

1 FL OUNCE = 30 ML

1 CUP = 237 ML

1 PINT (2 CUPS) = 473 ML

1 QUART (4 CUPS) = .95 LITER

1 GALLON (16 CUPS) = 3.8 LITERS

1 OZ = 28 GRAMS

1 POUND = 454 GRAMS

BUTTER

1 CUP BUTTER = 2 STICKS = 8 OUNCES = 230 GRAMS = 8 TABLESPOONS

WHAT DOES 1 CUP EQUAL

1 CUP = 8 FLUID OUNCES

1 CUP = 16 TABLESPOONS

1 CUP = 48 TEASPOONS

1 CUP = 1/2 PINT

1 CUP = 1/4 QUART

1 CUP = 1/16 GALLON

1 CUP = 240 ML

BAKING PAN CONVERSIONS

1 CUP ALL-PURPOSE FLOUR = 4.5 OZ

1 CUP ROLLED OATS = 3 OZ 1 LARGE EGG = 1.7 OZ

1 CUP BUTTER = 8 OZ 1 CUP MILK = 8 OZ

1 CUP HEAVY CREAM = 8.4 OZ

1 CUP GRANULATED SUGAR = 7.1 OZ

1 CUP PACKED BROWN SUGAR = 7.75 OZ

1 CUP VEGETABLE OIL = 7.7 OZ

1 CUP UNSIFTED POWDERED SUGAR = 4.4 OZ

BAKING PAN CONVERSIONS

9-INCH ROUND CAKE PAN = 12 CUPS

10-INCH TUBE PAN =16 CUPS

11-INCH BUNDT PAN = 12 CUPS

9-INCH SPRINGFORM PAN = 10 CUPS

9 X 5 INCH LOAF PAN = 8 CUPS

9-INCH SQUARE PAN = 8 CUPS

Breakfast & Snacks And Fries Recipes

French Toast Slices

Servings: 1
Cooking Time:xx
Ingredients:

- 2 eggs
- 5 slices sandwich bread
- 100ml milk
- 2 tbsp flour
- 3 tbsp sugar
- 1 tsp ground cinnamon
- 1/2 tsp vanilla extract
- Pinch of salt

Directions:

1. Preheat your air fryer to 220ºC
2. Take your bread and cut it into three pieces of the same size
3. Take a mixing bowl and combine the other ingredients until smooth
4. Dip the bread into the mixture, coating evenly
5. Take a piece of parchment paper and lay it inside the air fryer
6. Arrange the bread on the parchment paper in one layer
7. Cook for 5 minutes
8. Turn and cook for another 5 minutes

Baba Ganoush

Servings: 4
Cooking Time:xx
Ingredients:

- 1 large aubergine/eggplant, sliced in half lengthways
- ½ teaspoon salt
- 5 tablespoons olive oil
- 1 bulb garlic
- 30 g/2 tablespoons tahini or nut butter
- 2 tablespoons freshly squeezed lemon juice
- ½ teaspoon ground cumin
- ¼ teaspoon smoked paprika
- salt and freshly ground black pepper
- 3 tablespoons freshly chopped flat-leaf parsley

Directions:

1. Preheat the air-fryer to 200ºC/400ºF.
2. Lay the aubergine/eggplant halves cut side up. Sprinkle over the salt, then drizzle over 1 tablespoon of oil. Cut the top off the garlic bulb, brush the exposed cloves with a little olive oil, then wrap in foil. Place the aubergine/eggplant and foil-wrapped garlic in the preheated air-fryer and air-fry for 15–20 minutes until the inside of the aubergine is soft and buttery in texture.
3. Scoop the flesh of the aubergine into a bowl. Squeeze out about 1 tablespoon of the cooked garlic and add to the bowl with the remaining 4 tablespoons of olive oil, the tahini/nut butter, lemon juice, spices and salt and pepper to taste. Mix well and serve with fresh flat-leaf parsley sprinkled over.

Meaty Egg Cups

Servings: 4
Cooking Time:xx

Ingredients:

- 8 slices of toasted sandwich bread
- 2 slices of ham
- 4 eggs
- Salt and pepper to taste
- Butter for greasing

Directions:

1. Take 4 ramekins and grease the insides with a little butter
2. Flatten the slices of toast with a rolling pin and arrange inside the ramekins - two in each
3. Line the inside of each ramekin with a slice of ham
4. Crack one egg into each ramekin
5. Season with a little salt and pepper
6. Place the ramekins into the air fryer and cook at 160ºC for 15 minutes
7. Remove from the fryer and wait to cool just slightly
8. Remove and serve

Pitta Pizza

Servings: 2
Cooking Time:xx

Ingredients:

- 2 round wholemeal pitta breads
- 3 tablespoons passata/strained tomatoes
- 4 tablespoons grated mozzarella
- 1 teaspoon dried oregano
- 1 teaspoon olive oil
- basil leaves, to serve

Directions:

1. Preheat the air-fryer to 200ºC/400ºF.
2. Pop the pittas into the preheated air-fryer and air-fry for 1 minute.
3. Remove the pittas from the air-fryer and spread a layer of the passata/strained tomatoes on the pittas, then scatter over the mozzarella, oregano and oil. Return to the air-fryer and air-fry for a further 4 minutes. Scatter over the basil leaves and serve immediately.

Plantain Fries

Servings: 2
Cooking Time:xx

Ingredients:

- 1 ripe plantain (yellow and brown outside skin)
- 1 teaspoon olive oil
- ¼ teaspoon salt

Directions:

1. Preheat the air-fryer to 180ºC/350ºF.
2. Peel the plantain and slice into fries about 6 x 1 cm/2½ x ½ in. Toss the fries in oil and salt, making sure every fry is coated.
3. Tip into the preheated air-fryer in a single layer (you may need to cook them in two batches, depending on the size of your air-fryer) and air-fry for 13–14 minutes until brown on the outside and soft on the inside. Serve immediately.

Easy Air Fryer Sausage

Servings: 5
Cooking Time:xx

Ingredients:

- 5 uncooked sausages
- 1 tbsp mustard
- Salt and pepper for seasoning

Directions:

1. Line the basket of your fryer with parchment paper
2. Arrange the sausages inside the basket
3. Set to 180°C and cook for 15 minutes
4. Turn the sausages over and cook for another 5 minutes
5. Remove and cool
6. Drizzle the mustard over the top and season to your liking

Sweet Potato Fries

Servings: 4
Cooking Time:xx

Ingredients:

- 2 medium sweet potatoes
- 2 teaspoons olive oil
- ½ teaspoon salt
- ½ teaspoon chilli/hot red pepper flakes
- ½ teaspoon smoked paprika

Directions:

1. Preheat the air-fryer to 190°C/375°F.
2. Peel the sweet potatoes and slice into fries about 1 x 1 cm/½ x ½ in. by the length of the potato. Toss the sweet potato fries in the oil, salt, chilli and paprika, making sure every fry is coated.
3. Tip into the preheated air-fryer in a single layer (you may need to cook them in two batches, depending on the size of your air-fryer). Air-fry for 10 minutes, turning once halfway during cooking. Serve immediately.

Muhammara

Servings: 4
Cooking Time:xx

Ingredients:

- 4 romano peppers
- 4 tablespoons olive oil
- 100 g/1 cup walnuts
- 90 g/1 heaped cup dried breadcrumbs (see page 9)
- 1 teaspoon cumin
- 2 tablespoons pomegranate molasses
- freshly squeezed juice of ½ a lemon
- ½ teaspoon chilli/chili salt (or salt and some chilli/hot red pepper flakes combined)
- fresh pomegranate seeds, to serve

Directions:

1. Preheat the air-fryer to 180°C/350°F.
2. Rub the peppers with ½ teaspoon of the olive oil. Add the peppers to the preheated air-fryer and air-fry for 8 minutes.
3. Meanwhile, lightly toast the walnuts by tossing them in a shallow pan over a medium heat for 3–5 minutes. Allow to cool, then grind the walnuts in a food processor. Once the peppers are cooked, chop off the tops and discard most of the seeds. Add to the food processor with all other ingredients. Process until smooth. Allow to cool in the fridge, then serve the dip with pomegranate seeds on top.

Blueberry Bread

Servings: 8
Cooking Time:xx

Ingredients:

- 260ml milk
- 3 eggs
- 25g protein powder
- 400g frozen blueberries
- 600g bisquick or pancake mixture

Directions:

1. Take a large mixing bowl and combine all ingredients until smooth
2. Preheat the air fryer to 250°C
3. Place the mixture into a loaf tin
4. Place the tin into the air fryer and cook for 30 minutes
5. A toothpick should come out clean if the bread is cooked

Whole Mini Peppers

Servings: 2
Cooking Time:xx

Ingredients:

- 9 whole mini (bell) peppers
- 1 teaspoon olive oil
- ¼ teaspoon salt

Directions:

1. Preheat the air-fryer to 180°C/350°F.
2. Place the peppers in a baking dish that fits in for your air-fryer and drizzle over the oil, then sprinkle over the salt.
3. Add the dish to the preheated air-fryer and air-fry for 10–12 minutes, depending on how 'chargrilled' you like your peppers.

Oozing Baked Eggs

Servings: 2
Cooking Time:xx

Ingredients:

- 4 eggs
- 140g smoked gouda cheese, cut into small pieces
- Salt and pepper to taste

Directions:

1. You will need two ramekin dishes and spray each one before using
2. Crack two eggs into each ramekin dish
3. Add half of the Gouda cheese to each dish
4. Season and place into the air fryer
5. Cook at 350°C for 15 minutes, until the eggs are cooked as you like them

Tangy Breakfast Hash

Servings: 6
Cooking Time:xx

Ingredients:

- 2 tbsp olive oil
- 2 sweet potatoes, cut into cubes
- 1 tbsp smoked paprika
- 1 tsp salt
- 1 tsp black pepper
- 2 slices of bacon, cut into small pieces

Directions:

1. Preheat your air fryer to 200ºC
2. Pour the olive oil into a large mixing bowl
3. Add the bacon, seasonings, potatoes and toss to evenly coat
4. Transfer the mixture into the air fryer and cook for 12-16 minutes
5. Stir after 10 minutes and continue to stir periodically for another 5 minutes

Healthy Breakfast Bagels

Servings: 2
Cooking Time:xx

Ingredients:

- 170g self raising flour
- 120ml plain yogurt
- 1 egg

Directions:

1. Take a large mixing bowl, combine the flour and the yogurt to create a dough
2. Cover a flat surface with a little extra flour and set the dough down
3. Create four separate and even balls
4. Roll each ball out into a rope shape and form a bagel with each
5. Take a small mixing bowl and whisk the egg
6. Brush the egg over the top of the bagel
7. Arrange the bagels inside your fryer evenly
8. Cook at 170ºC for 10 minutes
9. Allow to cool before serving

Blanket Breakfast Eggs

Servings: 2
Cooking Time:xx

Ingredients:

- 2 eggs
- 2 slices of sandwich bread
- Olive oil spray
- Salt and pepper to taste

Directions:

1. Preheat your air fryer to 190ºC and spray with a little oil
2. Meanwhile, take your bread and cut a hole into the middle of each piece
3. Place one slice inside your fryer and crack one egg into the middle
4. Season with a little salt and pepper
5. Cook for 5 minutes, before turning over and cooking for a further 2 minutes
6. Remove the first slice and repeat the process with the remaining slice of bread and egg

Potato Fries

Servings: 2
Cooking Time:xx

Ingredients:

- 2 large potatoes (baking potato size)
- 1 teaspoon olive oil
- salt

Directions:

1. Peel the potatoes and slice into fries about 5 x 1.5cm/¾ x ¾ in. by the length of the potato. Submerge the fries in a bowl of cold water and place in the fridge for about 10 minutes.
2. Meanwhile, preheat the air-fryer to 160ºC/325ºF.
3. Drain the fries thoroughly, then toss in the oil and season. Tip into the preheated air-fryer in a single layer (you may need to cook them in two batches, depending on the size of your air-fryer). Air-fry for 15 minutes, tossing once during cooking by shaking the air-fryer drawer, then increase the temperature of the air-fryer to 200ºC/400ºF and cook for a further 3 minutes. Serve immediately.

European Pancakes

Servings: 5
Cooking Time:xx

Ingredients:

- 3 large eggs
- 130g flour
- 140ml whole milk
- 2 tbsp unsweetened apple sauce
- A pinch of salt

Directions:

1. Set your fryer to 200ºC and add five ramekins inside to heat up
2. Place all your ingredients inside a blender to combine
3. Spray the ramekins with a little cooking spray
4. Pour the batter into the ramekins carefully
5. Fry for between 6-8 minutes, depending on your preference
6. Serve with your favourite toppings

Breakfast Eggs & Spinach

Servings: 4
Cooking Time:xx
Ingredients:

- 500g wilted, fresh spinach
- 200g sliced deli ham
- 1 tbsp olive oil
- 4 eggs
- 4 tsp milk
- Salt and pepper to taste
- 1 tbsp butter for cooking

Directions:

1. Preheat your air fryer to 180°C
2. You will need 4 small ramekin dishes, coated with a little butter
3. Arrange the wilted spinach, ham, 1 teaspoon of milk and 1 egg into each ramekin and season with a little salt and pepper
4. Place in the fryer 15 to 20 minutes, until the egg is cooked to your liking
5. Allow to cool before serving

Egg & Bacon Breakfast Cups

Servings: 8
Cooking Time:xx
Ingredients:

- 6 eggs
- 1 chopped red pepper
- 1 chopped green pepper
- 1 chopped yellow pepper
- 2 tbsp double cream
- 50g chopped spinach
- 50g grated cheddar cheese
- 50g grated mozzarella cheese
- 3 slices of cooked bacon, crumbled into pieces

Directions:

1. Take a large mixing bowl and crack the eggs
2. Add the cream and season with a little salt and pepper, combining everything well
3. Add the peppers, spinach, onions, both cheeses, and the crumbled bacon, combining everything once more
4. You will need silicone moulds or cups for this part, and you should pour equal amounts of the mixture into 8 cups
5. Cook at 150°C for around 12 or 15 minutes, until the eggs are cooked properly

Cumin Shoestring Carrots

Servings: 2
Cooking Time:xx

Ingredients:

- 300 g/10½ oz. carrots
- 1 teaspoon cornflour/cornstarch
- 1 teaspoon ground cumin
- ¼ teaspoon salt
- 1 tablespoon olive oil
- garlic mayonnaise, to serve

Directions:

1. Preheat the air-fryer to 200°C/400°F.
2. Peel the carrots and cut into thin fries, roughly 10 cm x 1 cm x 5 mm/4 x ½ x ¼ in. Toss the carrots in a bowl with all the other ingredients.
3. Add the carrots to the preheated air-fryer and air-fry for 9 minutes, shaking the drawer of the air-fryer a couple of times during cooking. Serve with garlic mayo on the side.

Courgette Fries

Servings: 2
Cooking Time:xx

Ingredients:

- 1 courgette/zucchini
- 3 tablespoons plain/all-purpose flour (gluten-free if you wish)
- ¼ teaspoon salt
- ¼ teaspoon freshly ground black pepper
- 60 g/¾ cup dried breadcrumbs (gluten-free if you wish; see page 9)
- 1 teaspoon dried oregano
- 20 g/¼ cup finely grated Parmesan
- 1 egg, beaten

Directions:

1. Preheat the air-fryer to 180°C/350°F.
2. Slice the courgette/zucchini into fries about 1.5 x 1.5 x 5 cm/⅝ x ⅝ x 2 in.
3. Season the flour with salt and pepper. Combine the breadcrumbs with the oregano and Parmesan.
4. Dip the courgettes/zucchini in the flour (shaking off any excess flour), then the egg, then the seasoned breadcrumbs.
5. Add the fries to the preheated air-fryer and air-fry for 15 minutes. They should be crispy on the outside but soft on the inside. Serve immediately.

Sauces & Snack And Appetiser Recipes

Korean Chicken Wings

Servings: 2
Cooking Time:xx
Ingredients:

- 25ml soy sauce
- 40g brown sugar
- 2 tbsp hot pepper paste
- 1 tsp sesame oil
- ½ tsp ginger paste
- ½ tsp garlic paste
- 2 green onions, chopped
- 400g chicken wings
- 1 tbsp vegetable oil

Directions:

1. Preheat air fryer to 200°C
2. Place all ingredients apart from chicken wings and vegetable oil in a pan and simmer for about 4 minutes set aside
3. Massage the vegetable oil into the chicken wings
4. Place in the air fryer and cook for about 10 minutes
5. Turn and cook for a further 10 minutes
6. Coat the wings in the sauce and return to the air fryer
7. Cook for about 2 minutes

Garlic Cheese Bread

Servings: 2
Cooking Time:xx
Ingredients:

- 250g grated mozzarella
- 50g grated parmesan
- 1 egg
- ½ tsp garlic powder

Directions:

1. Line air fryer with parchment paper
2. Mix ingredients in a bowl
3. Press into a circle onto the parchment paper in the air fryer
4. Heat the air fryer to 175°C
5. Cook for 10 minutes

Spring Rolls

Servings: 20
Cooking Time:xx

Ingredients:

- 160g dried rice noodles
- 1 tsp sesame oil
- 300g minced beef
- 200g frozen vegetables
- 1 onion, diced
- 3 cloves garlic, crushed
- 1 tsp soy sauce
- 1 tbsp vegetable oil
- 1 pack egg roll wrappers

Directions:

1. Soak the noodles in a bowl of water until soft
2. Add the minced beef, onion, garlic and vegetables to a pan and cook for 6 minutes
3. Remove from the heat, stir in the noodles and add the soy
4. Heat the air fryer to 175ºC
5. Add a diagonal strip of filling in each egg roll wrapper
6. Fold the top corner over the filling, fold in the two side corners
7. Brush the centre with water and roll to seal
8. Brush with vegetable oil, place in the air fryer and cook for about 8 minutes until browned

Jalapeño Pockets

Servings: 4
Cooking Time:xx

Ingredients:

- 1 chopped onion
- 60g cream cheese
- 1 jalapeño, chopped
- 8 wonton wrappers
- ¼ tsp garlic powder
- ⅛ tsp onion powder

Directions:

1. Cook the onion in a pan for 5 minutes until softened
2. Add to a bowl and mix with the remaining ingredients
3. Lay the wonton wrappers out and add filling to each one
4. Fold over to create a triangle and seal with water around the edges
5. Heat the air fryer to 200ºC
6. Place in the air fryer and cook for about 4 minutes

Italian Rice Balls

Servings: 2
Cooking Time:xx

Ingredients:

- 400g cooked rice
- 25g breadcrumbs, plus an extra 200g for breading
- 2 tbsp flour, plus an extra 2 tbsp for breading
- 1 tbsp cornstarch, plus an extra 3 tbsp for breading
- 1 chopped bell pepper
- 1 chopped onion
- 2 tbsp olive oil
- 1 tsp red chilli flakes
- 5 chopped mozzarella cheese sticks
- A little water for the breading
- Salt and pepper for seasoning

Directions:

1. Place the cooked rice into a bowl and mash with a fork. Place to one side
2. Take a saucepan and add the oil, salting the onion and peppers until they're both soft
3. Add the chilli flakes and a little salt and combine
4. Add the mixture to the mashed rice and combine
5. Add the 2 tbsp flour and 1 tbsp cornstarch, along with the 25g breadcrumbs and combine well
6. Use your hands to create balls with the mixture
7. Stuff a piece of the mozzarella inside the balls and form around it
8. Take a bowl and add the rest of the flour, corn starch and a little seasoning, with a small amount of water to create a thick batter
9. Take another bowl and add the rest of the breadcrumbs
10. Dip each rice ball into the batter and then the breadcrumbs
11. Preheat the air fryer to 220ºC
12. Cook for 6 minutes, before shaking and cooking for another 6 minutes

Waffle Fries

Servings: 4
Cooking Time:xx

Ingredients:

- 2 large potatoes, russet potatoes work best
- 1 tsp salt for seasoning
- Waffle cutter

Directions:

1. Peel the potatoes and slice using the waffle cutter. You can also use a mandolin cutter that has a blade
2. Transfer the potatoes to a bowl and season with the salt, coating evenly
3. Add to the air fryer and cook at 220ºC for 15 minutes, shaking every so often

Pepperoni Bread

Servings: 4
Cooking Time:xx
Ingredients:

- Cooking spray
- 400g pizza dough
- 200g pepperoni
- 1 tbsp dried oregano
- Ground pepper to taste
- Garlic salt to taste
- 1 tsp melted butter
- 1 tsp grated parmesan
- 50g grated mozzarella

Directions:

1. Line a baking tin with 2 inch sides with foil to fit in the air fryer
2. Spray with cooking spray
3. Preheat the air fryer to 200ºC
4. Roll the pizza dough into 1 inch balls and line the baking tin
5. Sprinkle with pepperoni, oregano, pepper and garlic salt
6. Brush with melted butter and sprinkle with parmesan
7. Place in the air fryer and cook for 15 minutes
8. Sprinkle with mozzarella and cook for another 2 minutes

Spicy Egg Rolls

Servings: 4
Cooking Time:xx
Ingredients:

- 1 rotisserie chicken, shredded and diced
- 3 tbsp water
- 3 tbsp taco seasoning
- 1 can of black beans, drained
- 1 red bell pepper, diced
- 1 can of sweetcorn, drained
- 1 jalapeño pepper, deseeded and minced
- 2 packs of egg roll wrappers
- 250g grated strong cheddar cheese
- 250g grated Monterey Jack cheese

Directions:

1. Take a medium bowl and add the water and taco seasoning, combining well
2. Add the shredded check and coat well
3. Lay out an egg roll wrapper and arrange it so that one corner is facing towards you
4. Add 3 tablespoons of the mixture into the wrapper, just below the middle
5. Roll the corner facing you upwards, pulling it tightly closed over the mixture
6. Add a little water to the other two corners and fold into the centre and pat down to seal
7. Roll the rest of the wrapper up, so that all the corners are sealed
8. Repeat with the rest of the mixture
9. Preheat the air fryer to 220ºC
10. Cook for 9 minutes and turn over at the halfway point

Snack Style Falafel

Servings: 15
Cooking Time:xx

Ingredients:

- 150g dry garbanzo beans
- 300g coriander
- 75g flat leaf parsley
- 1 red onion, quartered
- 1 clove garlic
- 2 tbsp chickpea flour
- Cooking spray
- 1 tbsp cumin
- 1 tbsp coriander
- 1 tbsp sriracha
- ½ tsp baking powder
- Salt and pepper to taste
- ¼ tsp baking soda

Directions:

1. Add all ingredients apart from the baking soda and baking powder to a food processor and blend well
2. Cover and rest for 1 hour
3. Heat air fryer to 190ºC
4. Add baking powder and baking soda to mix and combine
5. Form mix into 15 equal balls
6. Spray air fryer with cooking spray
7. Add to air fryer and cook for 8-10 minutes

Asian Devilled Eggs

Servings: 12
Cooking Time:xx

Ingredients:

- 6 large eggs
- 2 tbsp mayo
- 1 ½ tsp sriracha
- 1 ½ tsp sesame oil
- 1 tsp soy sauce
- 1 tsp dijon mustard
- 1 tsp finely grated ginger
- 1 tsp rice vinegar
- 1 chopped green onion
- Toasted sesame seeds

Directions:

1. Set air fryer to 125ºC
2. Place eggs in the air fryer and cook for 15 minutes
3. Remove from the air fryer and place in a bowl of iced water for 10 minutes
4. Peel and cut in half
5. Scoop out the yolks and place in a food processor
6. Add the ingredients apart from the sesame seeds and green onion and combine until smooth
7. Place in a piping bag and pipe back into the egg whites
8. Garnish with seeds and green onion

Potato Patties

Servings: 12
Cooking Time:xx

Ingredients:

- 150g instant mash
- 50g peas and carrots
- 2 tbsp coriander
- 1 tbsp oil
- 100ml hot water
- ½ tsp turmeric
- ½ tsp cayenne
- ½ tsp salt
- ½ tsp cumin seeds
- ¼ tsp ground cumin

Directions:

1. Place all the ingredients in a bowl. Mix well cover and stand for 10 minutes
2. Preheat the air fryer to 200ºC
3. Spray the air fryer with cooking spray
4. Make 12 patties, place in the air fryer and cook for 10 minutes

Jalapeño Poppers

Servings: 2
Cooking Time:xx

Ingredients:

- 10 jalapeños, halved and deseeded
- 100g cream cheese
- 50g parsley
- 150g breadcrumbs

Directions:

1. Mix 1/2 the breadcrumbs with the cream cheese
2. Add the parsley
3. Stuff the peppers with the cream cheese mix
4. Top the peppers with the remaining breadcrumbs
5. Heat the air fryer to 185ºC
6. Place in the air fryer and cook for 6-8 minutes

Tostones

Servings: 4
Cooking Time:xx

Ingredients:

- 2 unripe plantains
- Olive oil cooking spray
- 300ml of water
- Salt to taste

Directions:

1. Preheat the air fryer to 200ºC
2. Slice the tips off the plantain
3. Cut the plantain into 1 inch chunks
4. Place in the air fryer spray with oil and cook for 5 minutes
5. Remove the plantain from the air fryer and smash to ½ inch pieces
6. Soak in a bowl of salted water
7. Remove from the water and return to the air fryer season with salt cook for 5 minutes
8. Turn and cook for another 5 minutes

Corn Nuts

Servings: 8
Cooking Time:xx

Ingredients:

- 1 giant white corn
- 3 tbsp vegetable oil
- 2 tsp salt

Directions:

1. Place the corn in a large bowl, cover with water and sit for 8 hours
2. Drain, pat dry and air dry for 20 minutes
3. Preheat the air fryer to 200ºC
4. Place in a bowl and coat with oil and salt
5. Cook in the air fryer for 10 minutes shake then cook for a further 10 minutes

Scotch Eggs

Servings: 6
Cooking Time:xx

Ingredients:

- 300g pork sausage
- 6 hard boiled eggs, shelled
- 50g cup flour
- 2 eggs, beaten
- 1 cup breadcrumbs
- Cooking spray

Directions:

1. Divide sausage into 6 portions
2. Place an egg in the middle of each portion and wrap around the egg
3. Dip the sausage in flour, then egg and then coat in breadcrumbs
4. Place in the air fryer and cook at 200ºC for 12 minutes

Mozzarella Sticks

Servings: 4
Cooking Time:xx

Ingredients:

- 60ml water
- 50g flour
- 5 tbsp cornstarch
- 1 tbsp cornmeal
- 1 tsp garlic powder
- ½ tsp salt
- 100g breadcrumbs
- ½ tsp pepper
- ½ tsp parsley
- ½ tsp onion powder
- ¼ tsp oregano
- ½ tsp basil
- 200g mozzarella cut into ½ inch strips

Directions:

1. Mix water, flour, cornstarch, cornmeal, garlic powder and salt in a bowl
2. Stir breadcrumbs, pepper, parsley, onion powder, oregano and basil together in another bowl
3. Dip the mozzarella sticks in the batter then coat in the breadcrumbs
4. Heat the air fryer to 200ºC
5. Cook for 6 minutes turn and cook for another 6 minutes

Onion Pakoda

Servings: 2
Cooking Time:xx

Ingredients:

- 200g gram flour
- 2 onions, thinly sliced
- 1 tbsp crushed coriander seeds
- 1 tsp chilli powder
- ¾ tsp salt
- ¼ tsp turmeric
- ¼ tsp baking soda

Directions:

1. Mix all the ingredients together in a large bowl
2. Make bite sized pakodas
3. Heat the air fryer to 200ºC
4. Line the air fryer with foil
5. Place the pakoda in the air fryer and cook for 5 minutes
6. Turn over and cook for a further 5 minutes

Onion Bahji

Servings: 8
Cooking Time:xx

Ingredients:

- 1 sliced red onion
- 1 sliced onion
- 1 tsp salt
- 1 minced jalapeño pepper
- 150g chickpea flour
- 4 tbsp water
- 1 clove garlic, minced
- 1 tsp coriander
- 1 tsp chilli powder
- 1 tsp turmeric
- ½ tsp cumin

Directions:

1. Place all ingredients in a bowl and mix well, leave to rest for 10 minutes
2. Preheat air fryer to 175ºC
3. Spray air fryer with cooking spray.
4. Form mix into bahji shapes and add to air fryer
5. Cook for 6 minutes turn and cook for a further 6 minutes

Pretzel Bites

Servings: 2
Cooking Time:xx

Ingredients:

- 650g flour
- 2.5 tsp active dry yeast
- 260ml hot water
- 1 tsp salt
- 4 tbsp melted butter
- 2 tbsp sugar

Directions:

1. Take a large bowl and add the flour, sugar and salt
2. Take another bowl and combine the hot water and yeast, stirring until the yeast has dissolved
3. Then, add the yeast mixture to the flour mixture and use your hands to combine
4. Knead for 2 minutes
5. Cover the bowl with a kitchen towel for around half an hour
6. Divide the dough into 6 pieces
7. Preheat the air fryer to 260ºC
8. Take each section of dough and tear off a piece, rolling it in your hands to create a rope shape, that is around 1” in thickness
9. Cut into 2” strips
10. Place the small dough balls into the air fryer and leave a little space in-between
11. Cook for 6 minutes
12. Once cooked, remove and brush with melted butter and sprinkle salt on top

Air-fried Pickles

Servings: 4
Cooking Time:xx

Ingredients:

- 1/2 cup mayonnaise
- 2 tsp sriracha sauce
- 1 jar dill pickle slices
- 1 egg
- 2 tbsp milk
- 50g flour
- 50g cornmeal
- ½ tsp seasoned salt
- ¼ tsp paprika
- ¼ tsp garlic powder
- ⅛ tsp pepper
- Cooking spray

Directions:

1. Mix the mayo and sriracha together in a bowl and set aside
2. Heat the air fryer to 200ºC
3. Drain the pickles and pat dry
4. Mix egg and milk together, in another bowl mix all the remaining ingredients
5. Dip the pickles in the egg mix then in the flour mix
6. Spray the air fryer with cooking spray
7. Cook for about 4 minutes until crispy

Poultry Recipes

Air Fryer Chicken Thigh Schnitzel

Servings: 4
Cooking Time:xx

Ingredients:

- 300g boneless chicken thighs
- 160g seasoned breadcrumbs
- 1 tsp salt
- ½ tsp ground black pepper
- 30g flour
- 1 egg
- Cooking spray

Directions:

1. Lay the chicken on a sheet of parchment paper and add another on top
2. Use a mallet or a rolling pin to flatten it down
3. Take a bowl and add the breadcrumbs with the salt and pepper
4. Place the flour into another bowl
5. Dip the chicken into the flour, then the egg, and then the breadcrumbs
6. Preheat air fryer to 190ºC
7. Place the chicken into the air fryer and spray with cooking oil
8. Cook for 6 minutes

Cheddar & Bbq Stuffed Chicken

Servings: 2
Cooking Time:xx

Ingredients:

- 3 strips of bacon
- 100g cheddar cheese
- 3 tbsp barbecue sauce
- 300g skinless and boneless chicken breasts
- salt and ground pepper to taste

Directions:

1. Preheat the air fryer to 190ºC
2. Cook one of the back strips for 2 minutes, before cutting into small pieces
3. Increase the temperature of the air fryer to 200ºC
4. Mix together the cooked bacon, cheddar cheese and 1 tbsp barbecue sauce
5. Take the chicken and make a pouch by cutting a 1 inch gap into the top
6. Stuff the pouch with the bacon and cheese mixture and then wrap around the chicken breast
7. Coat the chicken with the rest of the BBQ sauce
8. Cook for 10 minutes in the air fryer, before turning and cooking for an additional 10 minutes

Pizza Chicken Nuggets

Servings: 2
Cooking Time:xx

Ingredients:

- 60 g/¾ cup dried breadcrumbs (see page 9)
- 20 g/¼ cup grated Parmesan
- ½ teaspoon dried oregano
- ¼ teaspoon freshly ground black pepper
- 150 g/⅔ cup Mediterranean sauce (see page 102) or 150 g/5½ oz. jarred tomato pasta sauce (keep any leftover sauce for serving)
- 400 g/14 oz. chicken fillets

Directions:

1. Preheat the air-fryer to 180ºC/350ºF.
2. Combine the breadcrumbs, Parmesan, oregano and pepper in a bowl. Have the Mediterranean or pasta sauce in a separate bowl.
3. Dip each chicken fillet in the tomato sauce first, then roll in the breadcrumb mix until coated fully.
4. Add the breaded fillets to the preheated air-fryer and air-fry for 10 minutes. Check the internal temperature of the chicken has reached at least 74ºC/165ºF using a meat thermometer – if not, cook for another few minutes.
5. Serve with some additional sauce that has been warmed through.

Buffalo Wings

Servings: 4
Cooking Time:xx

Ingredients:

- 500g chicken wings
- 1 tbsp olive oil
- 5 tbsp cayenne pepper sauce
- 75g butter
- 2 tbsp vinegar
- 1 tsp garlic powder
- ¼ tsp cayenne pepper

Directions:

1. Preheat the air fryer to 182C
2. Take a large mixing bowl and add the chicken wings
3. Drizzle oil over the wings, coating evenly
4. Cook for 25 minutes and then flip the wings and cook for 5 more minutes
5. In a saucepan over a medium heat, mix the hot pepper sauce, butter, vinegar, garlic powder and cayenne pepper, combining well
6. Pour the sauce over the wings and flip to coat, before serving

Spicy Chicken Wing Drummettes

Servings: 4
Cooking Time:xx

Ingredients:

- 10 large chicken drumettes
- Cooking spray
- 100ml rice vinegar
- 3 tbsp honey
- 2 tbsp unsalted chicken stock
- 1 tbsp lower sodium soy sauce
- 1 tbsp toasted sesame oil
- ⅜ tsp crushed red pepper
- 1 garlic clove, finely chopped
- 2 tbsp chopped, unsalted, roasted peanuts
- 1 tbsp chopped fresh chives

Directions:

1. Coat the chicken in cooking spray and place inside the air fryer
2. Cook at 200°C for 30 minutes
3. Take a mixing bowl and combine the vinegar, honey, stock, soy sauce, oil, crushed red pepper and garlic
4. Cook to a simmer, until a syrup consistency is achieved
5. Coat the chicken in this mixture and sprinkle with peanuts and chives

Chicken Balls, Greek-style

Servings: 4
Cooking Time:xx

Ingredients:

- 500g ground chicken
- 1 egg
- 1 tbsp dried oregano
- 1.5 tbsp garlic paste
- 1 tsp lemon zest
- 1 tsp dried onion powder
- Salt and pepper to taste

Directions:

1. Take a bowl and combine all ingredients well
2. Use your hands to create meatballs - you should be able to make 12 balls
3. Preheat your air fryer to 260°C
4. Add the meatballs to the fryer and cook for 9 minutes

Nashville Chicken

Servings: 4
Cooking Time:xx

Ingredients:

- 400g boneless chicken breast tenders
- 2 tsp salt
- 2 tsp coarsely ground black pepper
- 2 tbsp hot sauce
- 2 tbsp pickle juice
- 500g all purpose flour
- 3 large eggs
- 300ml buttermilk
- 2 tbsp olive oil
- 6 tbsp cayenne pepper
- 3 tbsp dark brown sugar
- 1 tsp chilli powder
- 1 tsp garlic powder
- 1 tsp paprika
- Salt and pepper to taste

Directions:

1. Take a large mixing bowl and add the chicken, hot sauce, pickle juice, salt and pepper and combine
2. Place in the refrigerator for 3 hours
3. Transfer the flour to a bowl
4. Take another bowl and add the eggs, buttermilk and 1 tbsp of the hot sauce, combining well
5. Press each piece of chicken into the flour and coat well
6. Place the chicken into the buttermilk mixture and then back into the flour
7. Allow to sit or 10 minutes
8. Preheat the air fryer to 193C
9. Whisk together the spices, brown sugar and olive oil to make the sauce and pour over the chicken tenders
10. Serve whilst still warm

Chicken Tikka Masala

Servings: 4
Cooking Time:xx

Ingredients:

- 100g tikka masala curry pasta
- 200g low fat yogurt
- 600g skinless chicken breasts
- 1 tbsp vegetable oil
- 1 onion, chopped
- 400g can of the whole, peeled tomatoes
- 20ml water
- 1 tbsp sugar
- 2 tbsp lemon juice
- 1 small bunch of chopped coriander leaves

Directions:

1. Take a bowl and combine the tikka masala curry paste with half the yogurt
2. Cut the chicken into strips
3. Preheat the air fryer to 200°C
4. Add the yogurt mixture and coat the chicken until fully covered
5. Place into the refrigerator for 2 hours
6. Place the oil and onion in the air fryer and cook for 10 minutes
7. Add the marinated chicken, tomatoes, water and the rest of the yogurt and combine
8. Add the sugar and lemon juice and combine again
9. Cook for 15 minutes

Olive Stained Turkey Breast

Servings: 14
Cooking Time:xx

Ingredients:

- The brine from a can of olives
- 150ml buttermilk
- 300g boneless and skinless turkey breasts
- 1 sprig fresh rosemary
- 2 sprigs fresh thyme

Directions:

1. Take a mixing bowl and combine the olive brine and buttermilk
2. Pour the mixture over the turkey breast
3. Add the rosemary and thyme sprigs
4. Place into the refrigerator for 8 hours
5. Remove from the fridge and let the turkey reach room temperature
6. Preheat the air fryer to 175C
7. Cook for 15 minutes, ensuring the turkey is cooked through before serving

Chicken Fajitas

Servings: 3
Cooking Time:xx

Ingredients:

- 2 boneless chicken breasts, sliced into strips
- 5 mini (bell) peppers, sliced into strips
- 1 courgette/zucchini, sliced into 5-mm/¼-in. thick discs
- 2 tablespoons olive oil
- 28-g/1-oz. packet fajita seasoning mix
- TO SERVE
- wraps
- sliced avocado
- chopped tomato and red onion
- grated Red Leicester cheese
- plain yogurt
- coriander/cilantro
- lime wedges, for squeezing

Directions:

1. Combine the chicken, (bell) peppers, courgettes/zucchini and olive oil in a bowl. Add the fajita seasoning and stir to coat.
2. Preheat the air-fryer to 180ºC/350ºF.
3. Add the coated vegetables and chicken to the preheated air-fryer and air-fry for 12 minutes, shaking the drawer a couple of times during cooking. Check the internal temperature of the chicken has reached at least 74ºC/165ºF using a meat thermometer – if not, cook for another few minutes.
4. Serve immediately alongside the serving suggestions or your own choices of accompaniments.

Grain-free Chicken Katsu

Servings: 4
Cooking Time:xx

Ingredients:

- 125 g/1¼ cups ground almonds
- ½ teaspoon salt
- ½ teaspoon garlic powder
- ½ teaspoon dried parsley
- ½ teaspoon freshly ground black pepper
- ¼ teaspoon onion powder
- ¼ teaspoon dried oregano
- 450 g/1 lb. mini chicken fillets
- 1 egg, beaten
- oil, for spraying/drizzling
- coriander/cilantro leaves, to serve
- KATSU SAUCE
- 1 teaspoon olive oil or avocado oil
- 1 courgette/zucchini (approx. 150 g/5 oz.), finely chopped
- 1 carrot (approx. 100 g/3½ oz.), finely chopped
- 1 onion (approx. 120 g/4½ oz.), finely chopped
- 1 eating apple (approx. 150 g/5 oz.), cored and finely chopped
- 1 teaspoon ground ginger
- 1 teaspoon ground turmeric
- 2 teaspoons ground cumin
- 2 teaspoons ground coriander
- 1½ teaspoons mild chilli/chili powder
- 1 teaspoon garlic powder
- 1½ tablespoons runny honey
- 1 tablespoon soy sauce (gluten-free if you wish)
- 700 ml/3 cups vegetable stock (700 ml/3 cups water with 1½ stock cubes)

Directions:

1. First make the sauce. The easiest way to ensure all the vegetables and apple are finely chopped is to combine them in a food processor. Heat the oil in a large saucepan and sauté the finely chopped vegetables and apple for 5 minutes. Add all the seasonings, honey, soy sauce and stock and stir well, then bring to a simmer and simmer for 30 minutes.
2. Meanwhile, mix together the ground almonds, seasonings and spices. Dip each chicken fillet into the beaten egg, then into the almond-spice mix, making sure each fillet is fully coated. Spray the coated chicken fillets with olive oil (or simply drizzle over).
3. Preheat the air-fryer to 180ºC/350ºF.
4. Place the chicken fillets in the preheated air-fryer and air-fry for 10 minutes, turning halfway through cooking. Check the internal temperature of the chicken has reached at least 74ºC/165ºF using a meat thermometer – if not, cook for another few minutes.
5. Blend the cooked sauce in a food processor until smooth. Serve the chicken with the Katsu Sauce drizzled over (if necessary, reheat the sauce gently before serving) and scattered with coriander leaves. Any unused sauce can be frozen.

Quick Chicken Nuggets

Servings: 4
Cooking Time:xx

Ingredients:

- 500g chicken tenders
- 25g ranch salad dressing mixture
- 2 tbsp plain flour
- 100g breadcrumbs
- 1 egg, beaten
- Olive oil spray

Directions:

1. Take a large mixing bowl and arrange the chicken inside
2. Sprinkle the seasoning over the top and ensure the chicken is evenly coated
3. Place the chicken to one side for around 10 minutes
4. Add the flour into a resealable bag
5. Crack the egg into a small mixing bowl and whisk
6. Pour the breadcrumbs onto a medium sized plate
7. Transfer the chicken into the resealable bag and coat with the flour, giving it a good shake
8. Remove the chicken and dip into the egg, and then rolling it into the breadcrumbs, coating evenly
9. Repeat with all pieces of the chicken
10. Heat your air fryer to 200°C
11. Arrange the chicken inside the fryer and add a little olive oil spray to avoid sticking
12. Cook for 4 minutes, before turning over and cooking for another 4 minutes
13. Remove and serve whilst hot

Hawaiian Chicken

Servings: 2
Cooking Time:xx

Ingredients:

- 2 chicken breasts
- 1 tbsp butter
- A pinch of salt and pepper
- 160ml pineapple juice
- 25g brown sugar
- 3 tbsp soy sauce
- 2 tsp water
- 1 clove of garlic, minced
- 1 tsp grated ginger
- 2 tsp cornstarch

Directions:

1. Preheat the air fryer to 260°C
2. Take a bowl and combine the butter and salt and pepper
3. Cover the chicken with the butter and cook in the fryer for 15 minutes, turning halfway
4. Remove and allow to rest for 5 minutes
5. Take another bowl and mix together the pineapple juice, soy sauce, garlic, ginger, and brown sugar
6. Transfer to a saucepan and simmer for 5 minutes
7. Combine the water and cornstarch and add to the sauce, stirring continually for another minute
8. Slice the chicken into strips and pour the sauce over the top

Satay Chicken Skewers

Servings: 4
Cooking Time:xx
Ingredients:

- 3 chicken breasts, chopped into 3 x 3-cm/1¼ x 1¼-in. cubes
- MARINADE
- 200 ml/¾ cup canned coconut milk (including the thick part from the can)
- 1 plump garlic clove, finely chopped
- 2 teaspoons freshly grated ginger
- 2 tablespoons soy sauce
- 1 heaped tablespoon peanut butter
- 1 tablespoon maple syrup
- 1 tablespoon mild curry powder
- 1 tablespoon fish sauce

Directions:

1. Mix the marinade ingredients thoroughly in a bowl, then toss in the chopped chicken and stir to coat thoroughly. Leave in the fridge to marinate for at least 4 hours.
2. Preheat the air-fryer to 190°C/375°F.
3. Thread the chicken onto 8 metal skewers. Add to the preheated air-fryer (you may need to cook these in two batches, depending on the size of your air-fryer). Air-fry for 10 minutes. Check the internal temperature of the chicken has reached at least 74°C/165°F using a meat thermometer – if not, cook for another few minutes and then serve.

Smoky Chicken Breast

Servings: 2
Cooking Time:xx
Ingredients:

- 2 halved chicken breasts
- 2 tsp olive oil
- 1 tsp ground thyme
- 2 tsp paprika
- 1tsp cumin
- 0.5 tsp cayenne pepper
- 0.5 tsp onion powder
- Salt and pepper to taste

Directions:

1. In a medium bowl, combine the spices together
2. Pour the spice mixture onto a plate
3. Take each chicken breast and coat in the spices, pressing down to ensure an even distribution
4. Place the chicken to one side for 5 minutes
5. Preheat your air fryer to 180°C
6. Arrange the chicken inside the fryer and cook for 10 minutes
7. Turn the chicken over and cook for another 10 minutes
8. Remove from the fryer and allow to sit for 5 minutes before serving

Garlic Parmesan Fried Chicken Wings

Servings: 4
Cooking Time:xx

Ingredients:

- 16 chicken wing drumettes
- Cooking spray
- 240ml low fat buttermilk
- 150g flour
- 140g grated parmesan
- 2 tbsp low sodium soy sauce
- 1 sachet of your favourite chicken seasoning
- 1 tsp garlic powder
- Salt and pepper to taste

Directions:

1. Place the chicken onto a cooking tray and pour the soy sauce over the top, ensuring it is fully coated
2. Season the chicken and place in the refrigerator for 30 minutes
3. Add the flour and parmesan into a ziplock bag
4. Coat the chicken with buttermilk and add it to the ziplock bag with the flour
5. Preheat your air fryer to 200ºC
6. Place the chicken into the air fryer for 20 minutes
7. Shake the air fryer basket every 5 minutes until the 20 minutes is up

Honey Cajun Chicken Thighs

Servings: 6
Cooking Time:xx

Ingredients:

- 100ml buttermilk
- 1 tsp hot sauce
- 400g skinless, boneless chicken thighs
- 150g all purpose flour
- 60g tapioca flour
- 2.5 tsp cajun seasoning
- ½ tsp garlic salt
- ½ tsp honey powder
- ¼ tsp ground paprika
- ⅛ tsp cayenne pepper
- 4 tsp honey

Directions:

1. Take a large bowl and combine the buttermilk and hot sauce
2. Transfer to a plastic bag and add the chicken thighs
3. Allow to marinate for 30 minutes
4. Take another bowl and add the flour, tapioca flour, cajun seasoning, garlic, salt, honey powder, paprika, and cayenne pepper, combining well
5. Dredge the chicken through the mixture
6. Preheat the air fryer to 175C
7. Cook for 15 minutes before flipping the thighs over and cooking for another 10 minutes
8. Drizzle 1 tsp of honey over each thigh

Chicken And Cheese Chimichangas

Servings: 6
Cooking Time:xx

Ingredients:

- 100g shredded chicken (cooked)
- 150g nacho cheese
- 1 chopped jalapeño pepper
- 6 flour tortillas
- 5 tbsp salsa
- 60g refried beans
- 1 tsp cumin
- 0.5 tsp chill powder
- Salt and pepper to taste

Directions:

1. Take a large mixing bowl and add all of the ingredients, combining well
2. Add ⅓ of the filling to each tortilla and roll into a burrito shape
3. Spray the air fryer with cooking spray and heat to 200ºC
4. Place the chimichangas in the air fryer and cook for 7 minutes

Chicken And Wheat Stir Fry

Servings: 4
Cooking Time:xx

Ingredients:

- 1 onion
- 1 clove of garlic
- 200g skinless boneless chicken breast halves
- 3 whole tomatoes
- 400ml water
- 1 chicken stock cube
- 1 tbsp curry powder
- 130g wheat berries
- 1 tbsp vegetable oil

Directions:

1. Thinly slice the onion and garlic
2. Chop the chicken and tomatoes into cubes
3. Take a large saucepan and add the water, chicken stock, curry powder and wheat berries, combining well
4. Pour the oil into the air fryer bowl and heat for 5 minutes at 200ºC
5. Add the remaining ingredients and pour the contents into the air fryer
6. Cook for 15 minutes

Chicken Fried Rice

Servings: 4
Cooking Time:xx

Ingredients:

- 400g cooked white rice
- 400g cooked chicken, diced
- 200g frozen peas and carrots
- 6 tbsp soy sauce
- 1 tbsp vegetable oil
- 1 diced onion

Directions:

1. Take a large bowl and add the rice, vegetable oil and soy sauce and combine well
2. Add the frozen peas, carrots, diced onion and the chicken and mix together well
3. Pour the mixture into a nonstick pan
4. Place the pan into the air fryer
5. Cook at 182C for 20 minutes

Beef & Lamb And Pork Recipes

Mustard Pork Tenderloin

Servings: 2
Cooking Time:xx
Ingredients:

- 1 pork tenderloin
- 3 tbsp soy sauce
- 2 minced garlic cloves
- 3 tbsp olive oil
- 2 tbsp brown sugar
- 1 tbsp dijon mustard
- Salt and pepper for seasoning

Directions:

1. Take a bowl and combine the ingredients, except for the pork
2. Pour the mixture into a ziplock bag and then add the pork
3. Close the top and make sure the pork is well covered
4. Place in the refrigerator for 30minutes
5. Preheat your air fryer to 260°C
6. Remove the pork from the bag and place in the fryer
7. Cook for 25 minutes, turning halfway
8. Remove and rest for 5 minutes before slicing into pieces

Bbq Ribs

Servings: 2
Cooking Time:xx
Ingredients:

- 500g ribs
- 3 chopped garlic cloves
- 4 tbsp bbq sauce
- 1 tbsp honey
- ½ tsp five spice
- 1 tsp sesame oil
- 1 tsp salt
- 1 tsp black pepper
- 1 tsp soy sauce

Directions:

1. Chop the ribs into small pieces and place them in a bowl
2. Add all the ingredients into the bowl and mix well
3. Marinate for 4 hours
4. Preheat the air fryer to 180°C
5. Place the ribs into the air fryer and cook for 15 minutes
6. Coat the ribs in honey and cook for a further 15 minutes

Steak Popcorn Bites

Servings: 4
Cooking Time:xx

Ingredients:

- 500g steak, cut into 1" sized cubes
- 500g potato chips, ridged ones work best
- 100g flour
- 2 beaten eggs
- Salt and pepper to taste

Directions:

1. Place the chips into the food processor and pulse unit you get fine chip crumbs
2. Take a bowl and combine the flour with salt and pepper
3. Add the chips to another bowl and the beaten egg to another bowl
4. Take the steak cubes and dip first in the flour, then the egg and then the chip crumbs
5. Preheat your air fryer to 260ºC
6. Place the steak pieces into the fryer and cook for 9 minutes

Steak Fajitas

Servings: 4
Cooking Time:xx

Ingredients:

- 500g sliced steak
- 25g pineapple juice
- 2 tbsp lime juice
- 1 tbsp olive oil
- 1 tbsp soy sauce
- 1 tbsp minced garlic
- ½ tbsp chilli powder
- 1/2 tsp paprika
- 1 tsp cumin
- 1 pepper
- 1 onion
- Salt and pepper to taste

Directions:

1. Mix pineapple juice, lime juice, olive oil, soy sauce, garlic, cumin chilli powder and paprika. Pour over the steak and marinate for 4 hours
2. Line the air fryer with foil, add the peppers and onions, season with salt and pepper
3. Cook at 200ºC for 10 minutes, add the steak and cook for another 7 minutes
4. Serve with tortillas
5. Set your fryer to 170ºC and cook the sandwich for 4 minutes
6. Turn the sandwich over and cook for another 3 minutes
7. Turn the sandwich out and serve whilst hot
8. Repeat with the other remaining sandwich

Japanese Pork Chops

Servings: 4
Cooking Time:xx

Ingredients:

- 6 boneless pork chops
- 30g flour
- 2 beaten eggs
- 2 tbsp sweet chilli sauce
- 500g cup seasoned breadcrumbs
- ⅛ tsp salt
- ⅛ tsp pepper
- Tonkatsu sauce to taste

Directions:

1. Place the flour, breadcrumbs and eggs in 3 separate bowls
2. Sprinkle both sides of the pork with salt and pepper
3. Coat the pork in flour, egg and then breadcrumbs
4. Place in the air fryer and cook at 180ºC for 8 minutes, turn then cook for a further 5 minutes
5. Serve with sauces on the side

Breaded Bone-in Pork Chops

Servings: 2
Cooking Time:xx

Ingredients:

- 2 pork chops with the bone in
- 250g Italian breadcrumbs
- 2 tbsp mayonnaise
- 1/2 tsp garlic powder
- 1/2 tsp onion powder
- 1/2 tsp thyme
- 1/2 tsp paprika
- Salt and pepper to taste

Directions:

1. Preheat the air fryer to 260ºC
2. Take a large bowl and add the breadcrumbs, garlic powder, paprika, salt and pepper, and thyme, and onion powder, combining well
3. Cover the pork chops with the mayonnaise making sure to cover both sides
4. Coat the meat with the seasoning mixture, making sure it is fully covered
5. Cook the pork chops in the fryer for 10 minutes, turning over halfway

Southern Style Pork Chops

Servings: 4
Cooking Time:xx

Ingredients:

- 4 pork chops
- 3 tbsp buttermilk
- 100g flour
- Salt and pepper to taste
- Pork rub to taste

Directions:

1. Season the pork with pork rub
2. Drizzle with buttermilk
3. Coat in flour until fully covered
4. Place the pork chops in the air fryer, cook at 170ºC for 15 minutes
5. Turnover and cook for a further 10 minutes

Asparagus & Steak Parcels

Servings: 4
Cooking Time:xx
Ingredients:

- 500g flank steak, cut into 6 equal pieces
- 75ml Tamari sauce
- 2 crushed garlic cloves
- 250g trimmed asparagus
- 3 large bell peppers, thinly sliced
- 2 tbsp butter
- Salt and pepper to taste

Directions:

1. Season the steak to your liking
2. Place the meat in a zip top bag and add the Tamari and garlic, sealing the bag closed
3. Make sure the steaks are fully coated in the sauce and leave them in the fright at least 1 hour, but preferably overnight
4. Remove the steaks from the bag and throw the marinade away
5. Place the peppers and sliced asparagus in the centre of each steak piece
6. Roll the steak up and secure in place with a tooth pick
7. Preheat your air fryer to 250ºC
8. Transfer the meat parcels to the air fryer and cook for 5 minutes
9. Allow to rest before serving
10. Melt the butter in a saucepan, over a medium heat, adding the juices from the air fryer
11. Combine well and keep cooking until thickened
12. Pour the sauce over the steak parcels and season to your liking

Air Fryer Pork Bratwurst

Servings: 2
Cooking Time:xx
Ingredients:

- 2 pork bratwursts
- 2 hotdog bread rolls
- 2 tbsp tomato sauce

Directions:

1. Preheat the air fryer to 200ºC
2. Place the bratwurst in the fryer and cook for 10 minutes, turning halfway
3. Remove and place in the open bread rolls
4. Place back into the air fryer for 1 to 2 minutes, until the read is slightly crisped
5. Enjoy with the tomato sauce either on top or on the side

Vegetable & Beef Frittata

Servings: 2
Cooking Time:xx

Ingredients:

- 250g ground beef
- 4 shredded hash browns
- 8 eggs
- Half a diced onion
- 1 courgette, diced
- 250g grated cheese
- Salt and pepper for seasoning

Directions:

1. Break the ground beef up and place in the air fryer
2. Add the onion and combine well
3. Cook at 260°C for 3 minutes
4. Stir the mixture and cook foremother 2 minutes
5. Remove and clean the tray
6. Add the courgette to the air fryer and spray with a little cooking oil
7. Cook for 3 minutes
8. Add to the meat mixture and combine
9. Take a mixing bowl and combine the cheese, has browns, and eggs
10. Add the meat and courgette to the bowl and season with salt and pepper
11. Take a 6" round baking tray and add the mixture
12. Cook for 8 minutes before cutting lines in the top and cooking for another 8 minutes
13. Cut into slices before serving

Cheesy Meatball Sub

Servings: 2
Cooking Time:xx

Ingredients:

- 8 frozen pork meatballs
- 5 tbsp marinara sauce
- 160g grated parmesan cheese
- 2 sub rolls or hotdog rolls
- 1/4 tsp dried oregano

Directions:

1. Preheat the air fryer to 220°C
2. Place the meatball in the air fryer and cook for around 10 minutes, turning halfway through
3. Place the marinara sauce in a bowl
4. Add the meatballs to the sauce and coat completely
5. Add the oregano on top and coat once more
6. Take the bread roll and add the mixture inside
7. Top with the cheese
8. Place the meatball sub back in the air fryer and cook for 2 minutes until the bad is toasted and the cheese has melted

Cheeseburger Egg Rolls

Servings: 4
Cooking Time:xx

Ingredients:

- 400g minced beef
- ¼ tsp garlic powder
- ¼ tsp onion powder
- 1 chopped red pepper
- 1 chopped onion
- 6 dill pickles, chopped
- Salt and pepper
- 3 tbsp grated cheese
- 3 tbsp cream cheese
- 2 tbsp ketchup
- 1 tbsp mustard
- 6 large egg roll wrappers

Directions:

1. Cook the pepper, onion and minced beef in a pan for about 5 minutes
2. Remove from heat and stir in cheese, cream cheese, ketchup and mustard
3. Put the mix into a bowl and stir in the pickles
4. Place ⅙ of the mix in the centre of each wrap, moisten the edges with water roll up the wrap around the mixture and seal
5. Set your fryer to 200°C and cook for about 7 minutes
6. Turn the sandwich over and cook for another 3 minutes
7. Turn the sandwich out and serve whilst hot
8. Repeat with the other remaining sandwich

Taco Lasagne Pie

Servings: 4
Cooking Time:xx

Ingredients:

- 450g ground beef
- 2 tbsp olive oil
- 1 chopped onion
- 1 minced garlic clove
- 1 tsp cumin
- 1 tsp oregano
- 1/2 tsp adobo
- 266g grated Cheddar cheese
- 4 flour tortillas
- 112g tomato sauce

Directions:

1. Soften the onions with the olive oil in a frying pan
2. Add the beef and garlic until the meat has browned
3. Add the tomato sauce, cumin, oregano, and adobo and combine
4. Allow to simmer for a few minutes
5. Place one tortilla on the bottom of your air fryer basket
6. Add a meat layer, followed by a layer of the cheese, and continue alternating this routine until you have no meat left
7. Add a tortilla on top and sprinkle with the rest of the cheese
8. Cook at 180°C for 8 minutes

Beef Fried Rice

Servings: 2
Cooking Time:xx

Ingredients:

- 400g cooked rice
- 250g cooked beef strips
- 1 tbsp sesame oil
- 1 diced onion
- 1 egg
- 2 tsp garlic powder
- Salt and pepper
- 1 tbsp vegetable oil
- 250g frozen peas

Directions:

1. Preheat air fryer to 175ºC
2. Season the beef with salt, pepper and garlic powder, cook in a pan until about ¾ cooked
3. Mix the rice with peas carrots and vegetable oil, add the beef and mix
4. Add to the air fryer and cook for about 10 minutes
5. Add the egg and cook until the egg is done

Honey & Mustard Meatballs

Servings: 4
Cooking Time:xx

Ingredients:

- 500g minced pork
- 1 red onion
- 1 tsp mustard
- 2 tsp honey
- 1 tsp garlic puree
- 1 tsp pork seasoning
- Salt and pepper

Directions:

1. Thinly slice the onion
2. Place all the ingredients in a bowl and mix until well combined
3. Form into meatballs, place in the air fryer and cook at 180ºC for 10 minutes

Beef Wellington

Servings: 4
Cooking Time:xx

Ingredients:

- 300g chicken liver pate
- 500g shortcrust pastry
- 600g beef fillet
- 1 egg beaten
- Salt and pepper

Directions:

1. Remove all the visible fat from the beef season with salt and pepper. Wrap in cling film and place in the fridge for 1 hour
2. Roll out the pastry, brush the edges with egg
3. Spread the pate over the pastry. Remove the clingfilm from the beef and place in the center of the pastry
4. Seal the pastry around the meat
5. Place in the air fryer and cook at 160ºC for 35 minutes

Sweet And Sticky Ribs

Servings:2
Cooking Time:1 Hour 15 Minutes

Ingredients:

- 500 g / 17.6 oz pork ribs
- 2 cloves garlic, minced
- 2 tbsp soy sauce
- 2 tsp honey
- 1 tbsp cayenne pepper
- 1 tsp olive oil
- 2 tbsp BBQ sauce
- 1 tsp salt
- 1 tsp black pepper

Directions:

1. Place the pork ribs on a clean surface and cut them into smaller chunks if necessary.
2. In a small mixing bowl, combine the minced garlic, soy sauce, 1 tsp honey, cayenne pepper, olive oil, BBQ sauce, salt, and pepper. Rub the pork ribs into the sauce and spice the mixture until fully coated.
3. Place the coated ribs in the fridge for 1 hour. Meanwhile, preheat the air fryer to 180 °C / 350 °F and line the bottom of the basket with parchment paper.
4. After one hour, transfer the pork ribs into the prepared air fryer basket. Close the lid and cook for 15 minutes, using tongs to turn them halfway through.
5. Once cooked, remove the ribs from the air fryer and use a brush to top each rib with the remaining 1 tsp honey.
6. Return the ribs to the air fryer for a further 2-3 minutes to heat the honey glaze before serving.

Italian Meatballs

Servings: 12
Cooking Time:xx

Ingredients:

- 2 tbsp olive oil
- 2 tbsp minced shallot
- 3 cloves garlic minced
- 100g panko crumbs
- 35g chopped parsley
- 1 tbsp chopped rosemary
- 60ml milk
- 400g minced pork
- 250g turkey sausage
- 1 egg beaten
- 1 tbsp dijon mustard
- 1 tbsp finely chopped thyme

Directions:

1. Preheat air fryer to 200ºC
2. Heat oil in a pan and cook the garlic and shallot over a medium heat for 1-2 minutes
3. Mix the panko and milk in a bowl and allow to stand for 5 minutes
4. Add all the ingredients to the panko mix and combine well
5. Shape into 1 ½ inch meatballs and cook for 12 minutes

Sausage Gnocchi One Pot

Servings: 2
Cooking Time:xx

Ingredients:

- 4 links of sausage
- 250g green beans, washed and cut into halves
- 1 tsp Italian seasoning
- 1 tbsp olive oil
- 300g gnocchi
- Salt and pepper for seasoning

Directions:

1. Preheat the air fryer to 220°C
2. Cut the sausage up into pieces
3. Take a bowl and add the gnocchi and green beans, along with the oil and season
4. Place the sausage into the fryer first and then the rest of the ingredients
5. Cook for 12 minutes, giving everything a stir halfway through

Tender Ham Steaks

Servings: 1
Cooking Time:xx

Ingredients:

- 1 ham steak
- 2 tbsp brown sugar
- 1 tsp honey
- 2 tbsp melted butter

Directions:

1. Preheat the air fryer to 220°C
2. Combine the melted butter and brown sugar until smooth
3. Add the ham to the air fryer and brush both sides with the butter mixture
4. Cook for 12 minutes, turning halfway through and re-brushing the ham
5. Drizzle honey on top before serving

Fish & Seafood Recipes

Garlic-parsley Prawns

Servings: 2
Cooking Time:xx
Ingredients:

- 300 g/10½ oz. raw king prawns/jumbo shrimp (without shell)
- 40 g/3 tablespoons garlic butter, softened (see page 72)
- 2 tablespoons freshly chopped flat-leaf parsley

Directions:

1. Thread the prawns/shrimp onto 6 metal skewers that will fit your air-fryer. Mix together the softened garlic butter and parsley and brush evenly onto the prawn skewers.
2. Preheat the air-fryer to 180ºC/350ºF.
3. Place the skewers on an air-fryer liner or a piece of pierced parchment paper. Add the skewers to the preheated air-fryer and air-fry for 2 minutes, then turn the skewers over and cook for a further 2 minutes. Check the internal temperature of the prawns has reached at least 50ºC/120ºF using a meat thermometer – if not, cook for another few minutes and serve.

Crispy Nacho Prawns

Servings: 6
Cooking Time:xx
Ingredients:

- 1 egg
- 18 large prawns
- 1 bag of nacho cheese flavoured corn chips, crushed

Directions:

1. Wash the prawns and pat dry
2. Place the chips into a bowl
3. In another bowl, whisk the egg
4. Dip the prawns into the egg and then the nachos
5. Preheat the air fryer to 180ºC
6. Cook for 8 minutes

Beer Battered Fish Tacos

Servings: 2
Cooking Time:xx
Ingredients:

- 300g cod fillets
- 2 eggs
- 1 can of Mexican beer
- 300g cornstarch
- 300g flour
- 2 soft corn tortillas
- ½ tsp chilli powder
- 1 tbsp cumin
- Salt and pepper to taste

Directions:

1. Whisk together the eggs and beer
2. In a separate bowl whisk together cornstarch, chilli powder, flour, cumin and salt and pepper
3. Coat the fish in the egg mixture then coat in flour mixture
4. Spray the air fryer with non stick spray and add the fish
5. Set your fryer to 170ºC and cook for 15 minutes
6. Place the fish in a corn tortilla

Mahi Fish Tacos

Servings: 4
Cooking Time:xx

Ingredients:

- 400g fresh mahi
- 8 small corn tortillas
- 2 tsp cajun seasoning
- 5 tbsp sour cream
- 2 tbsp mayonnaise
- 2 tbsp scotch bonnet pepper sauce (use 1 tbsp if you don't like your food too spicy)
- 1 tbsp sriracha sauce
- 2 tbsp lime juice
- Salt and pepper to taste
- 1 tbsp vegetable oil

Directions:

1. Clean the mahi. Cut into half inch slices and season with salt
2. Mix quarter parts cayenne pepper and black pepper with cajun seasoning. Sprinkle onto fish
3. Brush pepper sauce on both sides of the fish
4. Set the air fryer to 180ºC and cook for about 10 minutes or until golden brown
5. Whilst the fish cooks make the chipotle lime cream. Mix the mayo, sour cream, lime juice sriracha and cayenne pepper
6. Assemble tacos and enjoy

Pesto Salmon

Servings: 4
Cooking Time:xx

Ingredients:

- 4 x 150–175-g/5½–6-oz. salmon fillets
- lemon wedges, to serve
- PESTO
- 50 g/scant ½ cup toasted pine nuts
- 50 g/2 oz. fresh basil
- 50 g/⅔ cup grated Parmesan or Pecorino
- 100 ml/7 tablespoons olive oil

Directions:

1. To make the pesto, blitz the pine nuts, basil and Parmesan to a paste in a food processor. Pour in the olive oil and process again.
2. Preheat the air-fryer to 160ºC/325ºF.
3. Top each salmon fillet with 2 tablespoons of the pesto. Add the salmon fillets to the preheated air-fryer and air-fry for 9 minutes. Check the internal temperature of the fish has reached at least 63ºC/145ºF using a meat thermometer – if not, cook for another few minutes.

Peppery Lemon Shrimp

Servings: 2
Cooking Time:xx

Ingredients:

- 300g uncooked shrimp
- 1 tbsp olive oil
- 1 the juice of 1 lemon
- 0.25 tsp garlic powder
- 1 sliced lemon
- 1 tsp pepper
- 0.25 tsp paprika

Directions:

1. Heat the fryer to 200ºC
2. Take a medium sized mixing bowl and combine the lemon juice, pepper, garlic powder, paprika and the olive oil together
3. Add the shrimp to the bowl and make sure they're well coated
4. Arrange the shrimp into the basket of the fryer
5. Cook for between 6-8 minutes, until firm and pink

Furikake Salmon

Servings: 2
Cooking Time:xx

Ingredients:

- 1 salmon fillet
- 2 tbsp furikake
- 150ml mayonnaise
- 1 tbsp shoe
- Salt and pepper for seasoning

Directions:

1. Preheat the air fryer to 230ºC
2. Take a small bowl and combine the mayonnaise and shoyu
3. Add salt and pepper to the salmon on both sides
4. Place in the air fryer with the skin facing downwards
5. Brush a layer of the mayonnaise mixture on top of the salmon
6. Sprinkle the furikake on top
7. Cook for 10 minutes

Lemon Pepper Shrimp

Servings: 2
Cooking Time:xx

Ingredients:

- ½ tbsp olive oil
- The juice of 1 lemon
- ¼ tsp paprika
- 1 tsp lemon pepper
- ¼ tsp garlic powder
- 400g uncooked shrimp
- 1 sliced lemon

Directions:

1. Preheat air fryer to 200ºC
2. Mix olive oil, lemon juice, paprika, lemon pepper and garlic powder. Add the shrimp and mix well
3. Place shrimp in the air fryer and cook for 6-8 minutes until pink and firm.
4. Serve with lemon slices

Garlic Butter Salmon

Servings: 2
Cooking Time:xx

Ingredients:

- 2 salmon fillets, boneless with the skin left on
- 1 tsp minced garlic
- 2 tbsp melted butter
- 1 tsp chopped parsley
- Salt and pepper to taste

Directions:

1. Preheat the air fryer to 270 °C
2. Take a bowl and combine the melted butter, parsley and garlic to create a sauce
3. Season the salmon to your liking
4. Brush the salmon with the garlic mixture, on both sides
5. Place the salmon into the fryer, with the skin side facing down
6. Cook for 10 minutes - the salmon is done when it flakes with ease

Coconut Shrimp

Servings: 4
Cooking Time:xx

Ingredients:

- 250g flour
- 1 ½ tsp black pepper
- 2 eggs
- 150g unsweetened flaked coconut
- 1 Serrano chilli, thinly sliced
- 25g panko bread crumbs
- 300g shrimp raw
- ½ tsp salt
- 4 tbsp honey
- 25ml lime juice

Directions:

1. Mix together flour and pepper, in another bowl beat the eggs and in another bowl mix the panko and coconut
2. Dip each of the shrimp in the flour mix then the egg and then cover in the coconut mix
3. Coat the shrimp in cooking spray
4. Place in the air fryer and cook at 200ºC for 6-8 mins turning half way through
5. Mix together the honey, lime juice and chilli and serve with the shrimp

Gluten Free Honey And Garlic Shrimp

Servings: 2
Cooking Time:xx

Ingredients:

- 500g fresh shrimp
- 5 tbsp honey
- 2 tbsp gluten free soy sauce
- 2 tbsp tomato ketchup
- 250g frozen stir fry vegetables
- 1 crushed garlic clove
- 1 tsp fresh ginger
- 2 tbsp cornstarch

Directions:

1. Simmer the honey, soy sauce, garlic, tomato ketchup and ginger in a saucepan
2. Add the cornstarch and whisk until sauce thickens
3. Coat the shrimp with the sauce
4. Line the air fryer with foil and add the shrimp and vegetables
5. Cook at 180ºC for 10 minutes

Fish Sticks With Tartar Sauce Batter

Servings: 4
Cooking Time:xx

Ingredients:

- 6 tbsp mayonnaise
- 2 tbsp dill pickle
- 1 tsp seafood seasoning
- 400g cod fillets, cut into sticks
- 300g panko breadcrumbs

Directions:

1. Combine the mayonnaise, seafood seasoning and dill pickle in a large bowl.
2. Add the cod sticks and coat well
3. Preheat air fryer to 200ºC
4. Coat the fish sticks in the breadcrumbs
5. Place in the air fryer and cook for 12 minutes

Crispy Cajun Fish Fingers

Servings: 2
Cooking Time:xx

Ingredients:

- 350 g/12 oz. cod loins
- 1 teaspoon smoked paprika
- ½ teaspoon cayenne pepper
- ½ teaspoon onion granules
- ¾ teaspoon dried oregano
- ¼ teaspoon dried thyme
- ½ teaspoon salt
- ½ teaspoon unrefined sugar
- 40 g/½ cup dried breadcrumbs (gluten-free if you wish, see page 9)
- 2 tablespoons plain/all-purpose flour (gluten-free if you wish)
- 1 egg, beaten

Directions:

1. Slice the cod into 6 equal fish 'fingers'. Mix the spices, herbs, salt and sugar together, then combine with the breadcrumbs. Lay out three bowls: one with flour, one with beaten egg and one with the Cajun-spiced breadcrumbs. Dip each fish finger into the flour, then the egg, then the breadcrumbs until fully coated.
2. Preheat the air-fryer to 180°C/350°F.
3. Add the fish to the preheated air-fryer and air-fry for 6 minutes, until cooked inside. Check the internal temperature of the fish has reached at least 75°C/167°F using a meat thermometer – if not, cook for another few minutes.

Salt & Pepper Calamari

Servings: 2
Cooking Time:xx

Ingredients:

- 500g squid rings
- 500g panko breadcrumbs
- 250g plain flour
- 2 tbsp pepper
- 2 tbsp salt
- 200ml buttermilk
- 1 egg

Directions:

1. Take a medium bowl and combine the buttermilk and egg, stirring well
2. Take another bowl and combine the salt, pepper, flour, and panko breadcrumbs, combining again
3. Dip the quid into the buttermilk first and then the breadcrumbs, coating evenly
4. Place in the air fryer basket
5. Cook at 150°C for 12 minutes, until golden

Salmon Patties

Servings: 4
Cooking Time:xx

Ingredients:

- 400g salmon
- 1 egg
- 1 diced onion
- 200g breadcrumbs
- 1 tsp dill weed

Directions:

1. Remove all bones and skin from the salmon
2. Mix egg, onion, dill weed and bread crumbs with the salmon
3. Shape mixture into patties and place into the air fryer
4. Set air fryer to 180ºC
5. Cook for 5 minutes then turn them over and cook for a further 5 minutes until golden brown

Thai Salmon Patties

Servings: 7
Cooking Time:xx

Ingredients:

- 1 large can of salmon, drained and bones removed
- 30g panko breadcrumbs
- ¼ tsp salt
- 1 ½ tbsp Thai red curry paste
- 1 ½ tbsp brown sugar
- Zest of 1 lime
- 2 eggs
- Cooking spray

Directions:

1. Take a large bowl and combine all ingredients together until smooth
2. Use your hands to create patties that are around 1 inch in thickness
3. Preheat your air fryer to 180ºC
4. Coat the patties with cooking spray
5. Cook for 4 minutes each side

Fish In Foil

Servings: 2
Cooking Time:xx

Ingredients:

- 1 tablespoon avocado oil or olive oil, plus extra for greasing
- 1 tablespoon soy sauce (or tamari)
- 1½ teaspoons freshly grated garlic
- 1½ teaspoons freshly grated ginger
- 1 small red chilli/chile, finely chopped
- 2 skinless, boneless white fish fillets (about 350 g/12 oz. total weight)

Directions:

1. Mix the oil, soy sauce, garlic, ginger and chilli/chile together. Brush a little oil onto two pieces of foil, then lay the fish in the centre of the foil. Spoon the topping mixture over the fish. Wrap the foil around the fish to make a parcel, with a gap above the fish but shallow enough to fit in your air-fryer basket.
2. Preheat the air-fryer to 180ºC/350ºF.
3. Add the foil parcels to the preheated air-fryer and air-fry for 7–10 minutes, depending on the thickness of your fillets. The fish should just flake when a fork is inserted. Serve immediately.

Traditional Fish And Chips

Servings: 4
Cooking Time:xx

Ingredients:

- 4 potatoes, peeled and cut into chips
- 2 fish fillets of your choice
- 1 beaten egg
- 3 slices of wholemeal bread, grated into breadcrumbs
- 25g tortilla crisps
- 1 lemon rind and juice
- 1 tbsp parsley
- Salt and pepper to taste

Directions:

1. Preheat your air fryer to 200°C
2. Place the chips inside and cook until crispy
3. Cut the fish fillets into 4 slices and season with lemon juice
4. Place the breadcrumbs, lemon rind, parsley, tortillas and seasoning into a food processor and blitz to create a crumb consistency
5. Place the breadcrumbs on a large plate
6. Coat the fish in the egg and then the breadcrumb mixture
7. Cook for 15 minutes at 180°C

Garlic Tilapia

Servings: 2
Cooking Time:xx

Ingredients:

- 2 tilapia fillets
- 2 tsp chopped fresh chives
- 2 tsp chopped fresh parsley
- 2 tsp olive oil
- 1 tsp minced garlic
- Salt and pepper for seasoning

Directions:

1. Preheat the air fryer to 220°C
2. Take a small bowl and combine the olive oil with the chives, garlic, parsley and a little salt and pepper
3. Brush the mixture over the fish fillets
4. Place the fish into the air fryer and cook for 10 minutes, until flaky

Honey Sriracha Salmon

Servings: 2
Cooking Time:xx

Ingredients:

- 25g sriracha
- 25g honey
- 500g salmon fillets
- 1 tbsp soy sauce

Directions:

1. Mix the honey, soy sauce and sriracha, keep half the mix to one side for dipping
2. Place the salmon in the sauce skin side up and marinade for 30 minutes
3. Spray air fryer basket with cooking spray
4. Heat the air fryer to 200°C
5. Place salmon in the air fryer skin side down and cook for 12 minutes

Vegetarian & Vegan Recipes

Shakshuka

Servings: 2
Cooking Time:xx
Ingredients:

- 2 eggs
- BASE
- 100 g/3½ oz. thinly sliced (bell) peppers
- 1 red onion, halved and thinly sliced
- 2 medium tomatoes, chopped
- 2 teaspoons olive oil
- ¼ teaspoon salt
- ¼ teaspoon freshly ground black pepper
- ½ teaspoon chilli/hot red pepper flakes
- SAUCE
- 100 g/3½ oz. passata/strained tomatoes
- 1 tablespoon tomato purée/paste
- 1 teaspoon balsamic vinegar
- ½ teaspoon runny honey
- ½ teaspoon ground cumin
- ½ teaspoon paprika
- ¼ teaspoon salt
- ⅛ teaspoon freshly ground black pepper

Directions:

1. Preheat the air-fryer to 180°C/350°F.
2. Combine the base ingredients together in a baking dish that fits inside your air-fryer. Add the dish to the preheated air-fryer and air-fry for 10 minutes, stirring halfway through cooking.
3. Meanwhile, combine the sauce ingredients in a bowl. Pour this into the baking dish when the 10 minutes are up. Stir, then make a couple of wells in the sauce for the eggs. Crack the eggs into the wells, then cook for a further 5 minutes or until the eggs are just cooked and yolks still runny. Remove from the air-fryer and serve.

Macaroni & Cheese Quiche

Servings: 4
Cooking Time:xx
Ingredients:

- 8 tbsp macaroni pasta
- 1 block of short crust pastry
- 2 tbsp Greek yogurt
- 2 eggs
- 150ml milk
- 1 tsp garlic puree
- 400g grated cheese

Directions:

1. Rub the inside of 4 ramekins with flour
2. Line the ramekins with the pastry
3. Mix the yogurt, garlic and macaroni. Add to the ramekins until ¾ full
4. Mix the egg and milk together and pour over the macaroni. Sprinkle with cheese
5. Heat the air fryer to 180°C and cook for 20 minutes until golden brown.

Vegan Meatballs

Servings:4
Cooking Time:15 Minutes

Ingredients:

- 2 tbsp olive oil
- 2 tbsp soy sauce
- 1 onion, finely sliced
- 1 large carrot, peeled and grated
- 1 x 400 g / 14 oz can chickpeas, drained and rinsed
- 50 g / 1.8 oz plain flour
- 50 g / 1.8 oz rolled oats
- 2 tbsp roasted cashews, chopped
- 1 tsp garlic powder
- ½ tsp cumin

Directions:

1. Preheat the air fryer to 175 °C / 350 °F and line the air fryer with parchment paper or grease it with olive oil.
2. In a large mixing bowl, combine the olive oil and soy sauce. Add the onion slices and grated carrot and toss to coat in the sauce.
3. Place the vegetables in the air fryer and cook for 5 minutes until slightly soft.
4. Meanwhile, place the chickpeas, plain flour, rolled oats, and roasted cashews in a blender, and mix until well combined.
5. Remove the mixture from the blender and stir in the garlic powder and cumin. Add the onions and carrots to the bowl and mix well.
6. Scoop the mixture into small meatballs and place them into the air fryer. Increase the temperature on the machine up to 190 °C / 370 °F and cook the meatballs for 10-12 minutes until golden and crispy.

Saganaki

Servings: 2
Cooking Time:xx

Ingredients:

- 200 g/7 oz. kefalotyri or manouri cheese, sliced into wedges 1 cm/½ in. thick
- 2 tablespoons plain/all-purpose flour
- olive oil, for drizzling

Directions:

1. Preheat the air-fryer to 200°C/400°F.
2. Dip each wedge of cheese in the flour, then tap off any excess. Drizzle olive oil onto both sides of the cheese slices
3. Add the cheese to the preheated air-fryer and air-fry for 3 minutes. Remove from the air-fryer and serve.

Aubergine Dip

Servings: 4
Cooking Time:xx
Ingredients:

- 1 aubergine
- 2 tsp oil
- 3 tbsp tahini
- 1 tbsp lemon juice
- 1 clove garlic minced
- ⅛ tsp cumin
- ¼ tsp smoked salt
- ⅛ tsp salt
- Drizzle olive oil

Directions:

1. Cut the aubergine in half length wise and coat in oil, Place in the air fryer and cook at 200ºC for 20 minutes
2. Remove from the air fryer and allow to cool
3. Scoop out the aubergine from the peel and put in a food processor
4. Add all the remaining ingredients, blend to combine but not to a puree
5. Serve with a drizzle of olive oil

Cheese, Tomato & Pesto Crustless Quiches

Servings: 1–2
Cooking Time:xx
Ingredients:

- 40 g/½ cup grated mature Cheddar
- 3 eggs, beaten
- 3 cherry tomatoes, finely chopped
- salt and freshly ground black pepper
- ½ teaspoon olive oil, to grease ramekins
- 2 tablespoons pesto (jarred or see page 80)

Directions:

1. Preheat the air-fryer to 180ºC/350ºF.
2. Mix together the cheese, eggs, tomatoes, salt and pepper in a bowl.
3. Grease the ramekins with the oil (and line with parchment paper if you wish to remove the quiches to serve). Pour the egg mixture into the ramekins.
4. Place the ramekins in the preheated air-fryer and air-fry for 10 minutes, stirring the contents of the ramekins halfway through cooking. Serve hot with 1 tablespoon pesto drizzled over each quiche.

Stuffed Peppers

Servings: 6
Cooking Time:xx

Ingredients:

- 250g diced potatoes
- 100g peas
- 1 small onion, diced
- 1 carrot, diced
- 1 bread roll, diced
- 2 garlic cloves, minced
- 2 tsp mixed herbs
- 6 bell peppers
- 100g grated cheese

Directions:

1. Preheat air fryer to 180ºC
2. Combine all the ingredients together apart from the peppers
3. Stuff the peppers with the mix
4. Place in the air fryer and cook for about 20 minutes

Pakoras

Servings: 8
Cooking Time:xx

Ingredients:

- 200g chopped cauliflower
- 100g diced pepper
- 250g chickpea flour
- 30ml water
- ½ tsp cumin
- Cooking spray
- 1 onion, diced
- 1 tsp salt
- 1 garlic clove, minced
- 1 tsp curry powder
- 1 tsp coriander
- ½ tsp cayenne

Directions:

1. Preheat air fryer to 175ºC
2. Place all ingredients in a bowl and mix well
3. Spray cooking basket with oil
4. Spoon 2 tbsp of mix into the basket and flatten, continue until the basket is full
5. Cook for 8 minutes, turn then cook for a further 8 minutes

Roast Cauliflower & Broccoli

Servings: 6
Cooking Time:xx

Ingredients:

- 300g broccoli
- 300g cauliflower
- 2 tbsp oil
- ½ tsp garlic powder
- ¼ tsp salt
- ¼ tsp paprika
- ⅛ tsp pepper

Directions:

1. Preheat air fryer to 200ºC
2. Place broccoli and cauliflower in a bowl and microwave for 3 minutes
3. Add remaining ingredients and mix well
4. Add to the air fryer and cook for about 12 mins

Tofu Bowls

Servings: 4
Cooking Time:xx

Ingredients:

- 1 block of tofu, cut into cubes
- 40ml soy sauce
- 2 tbsp sesame oil
- 1 tsp garlic powder
- 1 chopped onion
- 2 tbsp Tahini dressing
- 3 bunches baby bok choy, chopped
- 300g quinoa
- 1 medium cucumber, sliced
- 1 cup shredded carrot
- 1 avocado, sliced

Directions:

1. Mix the soy sauce, 1 tbsp sesame oil and garlic powder in a bowl. Add the tofu marinade for 10 minutes
2. Place in the air fryer and cook at 200ºC for 20 minutes turning halfway
3. Heat the remaining sesame oil in a pan and cook the onions for about 4 minutes
4. Add the bok choy and cook for another 4 minutes
5. Divide the quinoa between your bowls add bok choy, carrot, cucumber and avocado. Top with the tofu and drizzle with Tahini

Radish Hash Browns

Servings: 4
Cooking Time:xx

Ingredients:

- 300g radish
- 1 onion
- 1 tsp onion powder
- ¾ tsp sea salt
- ½ tsp paprika
- ¼ tsp ground black pepper
- 1 tsp coconut oil

Directions:

1. Wash the radish, trim off the roots and slice in a processor along with the onions
2. Add the coconut oil and mix well
3. Put the onions and radish into the air fryer and cook at 180ºC for 8 minutes shaking a few times
4. Put the onion and radish in a bowl add seasoning and mix well
5. Put back in the air fryer and cook at 200ºC for 5 minutes

Spinach And Egg Air Fryer Breakfast Muffins

Servings:4
Cooking Time:10 Minutes

Ingredients:

- 8 eggs
- 100 g / 3.5 oz fresh spinach
- 50 g / 1.8 oz cheddar cheese, grated
- ½ onion, finely sliced
- 1 tsp black pepper

Directions:

1. Preheat your air fryer to 200 °C / 400 °F and line an 8-pan muffin tray with parchment paper or grease with olive oil.
2. Gently press the spinach leaves into the bottom of each prepared muffin cup.
3. Sprinkle the finely sliced onion on top of the spinach.
4. Crack 2 eggs into each cup on top of the spinach and add some of the grated cheddar cheese on top of the eggs. Top with a light sprinkle of black pepper.
5. Carefully place the muffins into the air fryer basket and shut the lid. Bake for 10 minutes until the eggs are set and the muffins are hot throughout.
6. Serve the muffins while still hot for breakfast.

Tempura Veggies

Servings: 4
Cooking Time:xx

Ingredients:

- 150g flour
- ½ tsp salt
- ½ tsp pepper
- 2 eggs
- 2 tbsp cup water
- 100g avocado wedges
- 100g courgette slices
- 100g panko breadcrumbs
- 2 tsp oil
- 100g green beans
- 100g asparagus spears
- 100g red onion rings
- 100g pepper rings

Directions:

1. Mix together flour, salt and pepper. In another bowl mix eggs and water
2. Stir together panko crumbs and oil in a separate bowl
3. Dip vegetables in the flour mix, then egg and then the bread crumbs
4. Preheat the air fryer to 200ºC
5. Place in the air fryer and cook for about 10 minutes until golden brown

Roasted Cauliflower

Servings: 2
Cooking Time:xx

Ingredients:

- 3 cloves garlic
- 1 tbsp peanut oil
- ½ tsp salt
- ½ tsp paprika
- 400g cauliflower florets

Directions:

1. Preheat air fryer to 200ºC
2. Crush the garlic, place all ingredients in a bowl and mix well
3. Place in the air fryer and cook for about 15 minutes, shaking every 5 minutes

Spanakopita Bites

Servings: 4
Cooking Time:xx

Ingredients:

- 300g baby spinach
- 2 tbsp water
- 100g cottage cheese
- 50g feta cheese
- 2 tbsp grated parmesan
- 1 tbsp olive oil
- 4 sheets of filo pastry
- 1 large egg white
- 1 tsp lemon zest
- 1 tsp oregano
- ¼ tsp salt
- ¼ tsp pepper
- ⅛ tsp cayenne

Directions:

1. Place spinach in water and cook for about 5 minutes, drain
2. Mix all ingredients together
3. Place a sheet of pastry down and brush with oil, place another on the top and do the same, continue until all four on top of each other
4. Ut the pastry into 8 strips then cut each strip in half across the middle
5. Add 1 tbsp of mix to each piece of pastry
6. Fold one corner over the mix to create a triangle, fold over the other corner to seal
7. Place in the air fryer and cook at 190ºC for about 12 minutes until golden brown

Bbq Sandwich

Servings: 2
Cooking Time:xx

Ingredients:

- 1 tbsp mayo
- ¼ tsp white wine vinegar
- ¼ tsp lemon juice
- 1/8 tsp garlic powder
- Pinch of salt
- Cabbage mix
- 2 sandwich buns
- 150g bbq soy curls

Directions:

1. Mix mayo, white wine vinegar, lemon juice, cabbage mix, garlic powder and pinch of salt to make coleslaw. Set aside
2. Add the buns to the air fryer and cook at 200ºC for 5 minutes to toast
3. Fill the buns with coleslaw, soy curls, pickles and chopped onions

Whole Wheat Pizza

Servings: 2
Cooking Time:xx

Ingredients:

- 100g marinara sauce
- 2 whole wheat pitta
- 200g baby spinach leaves
- 1 small plum tomato, sliced
- 1 clove garlic, sliced
- 400g grated cheese
- 50g shaved parmesan

Directions:

1. Preheat air fryer to 160ºC
2. Spread each of the pitta with marinara sauce
3. Sprinkle with cheese, top with spinach, plum tomato and garlic. Finish with parmesan shavings
4. Place in the air fryer and cook for about 4 mins cheese has melted

Bagel Pizza

Servings: 1
Cooking Time:xx

Ingredients:

- 1 bagel
- 2 tbsp marinara sauce
- 6 slices vegan pepperoni
- 2 tbsp mozzarella
- Pinch of basil

Directions:

1. Heat the air fryer to 180ºC
2. Cut the bagel in half and toast for 2 minutes in the air fryer
3. Remove from the air fryer and top with marinara sauce, pepperoni and mozzarella
4. Return to the air fryer and cook for 4-5 minutes
5. Sprinkle with basil to serve

Ravioli Air Fryer Style

Servings: 4
Cooking Time:xx

Ingredients:

- Half a pack of frozen ravioli
- 200g Italian breadcrumbs
- 200ml buttermilk
- 5 tbsp marinara sauce
- 1 tbsp olive oil

Directions:

1. Preheat the air fryer to 220ºC
2. Place the buttermilk in a bowl
3. Add the breadcrumbs to another bowl
4. Take each piece of ravioli and dip it first into the buttermilk and then into the breadcrumbs, coating evenly
5. Add the ravioli to the air fryer and cook for 7 minutes, adding a small amount of oil at the halfway point
6. Serve with the marinara sauce on the side

Spicy Spanish Potatoes

Servings: 2
Cooking Time:xx

Ingredients:

- 4 large potatoes
- 1 tbsp olive oil
- 2 tsp paprika
- 2 tsp dried garlic
- 1 tsp barbacoa seasoning
- Salt and pepper

Directions:

1. Chop the potatoes into wedges
2. Place them in a bowl with olive oil and seasoning, mix well
3. Add to the air fryer and cook at 160ºC for 20 minutes
4. Shake, increase heat to 200ºC and cook for another 3 minutes

Side Dishes Recipes

Sweet & Spicy Baby Peppers

Servings: 2
Cooking Time:xx
Ingredients:

- 200 g/7 oz. piccarella (baby) peppers, deseeded and quartered lengthways
- 1 teaspoon olive oil
- ½ teaspoon chilli/chili paste
- ¼ teaspoon runny honey
- salt and freshly ground black pepper

Directions:

1. Preheat the air-fryer to 180ºC/350ºF.
2. Toss the peppers in the oil, chilli/chili paste and honey, then add salt and pepper to taste.
3. Place in the preheated air-fryer and air-fry for 6–8 minutes, depending on how 'chargrilled' you like them, turning them over halfway through.

Hasselback New Potatoes

Servings: 4
Cooking Time:xx
Ingredients:

- 8–12 new potatoes, roughly 5–7 cm/2–2¾ in. in length
- 2 teaspoons olive oil
- salt
- 1 tablespoon butter (optional)

Directions:

1. Preheat the air-fryer to 180ºC/350ºF.
2. Slice the potatoes multiple times widthways, making sure you do not cut all the way through (if you place the potatoes in the bowl of a wooden spoon to make these slices, it prevents you cutting all the way through). Coat the potatoes in the olive oil and sprinkle over the salt.
3. Add the potatoes to the preheated air-fryer and air-fry for 20–25 minutes until the potatoes are crispy on the outside but soft on the inside. Serve immediately.

Shishito Peppers

Servings: 2
Cooking Time:xx
Ingredients:

- 200g shishito peppers
- Salt and pepper to taste
- ½ tbsp avocado oil
- 75g grated cheese
- 2 limes

Directions:

1. Rinse the peppers
2. Place in a bowl and mix with oil, salt and pepper
3. Place in the air fryer and cook at 175ºC for 10 minutes
4. Place on a serving plate and sprinkle with cheese

Orange Tofu

Servings: 4
Cooking Time:xx

Ingredients:

- 400g tofu, drained
- 1 tbsp tamari
- 1 tbsp corn starch
- ¼ tsp pepper flakes
- 1 tsp minced ginger
- 1 tsp fresh garlic
- 1 tsp orange zest
- 75ml orange juice
- 75ml water
- 2 tsp cornstarch
- 1 tbsp maple syrup

Directions:

1. Cut the tofu into cubes, place in a bowl add the tamari and mix well
2. Mix in 1 tbsp starch and allow to marinate for 30 minutes
3. Place the remaining ingredients into another bowl and mix well
4. Place the tofu in the air fryer and cook at 190°C for about 10 minutes
5. Add tofu to a pan with sauce mix and cook until sauce thickens

Spicy Green Beans

Servings: 4
Cooking Time:xx

Ingredients:

- 300g green beans
- 1 tbsp sesame oil
- 1 tsp soy
- 1 tsp rice wine vinegar
- 1 clove garlic, minced
- 1 tsp red pepper flakes

Directions:

1. Preheat air fryer to 200°C
2. Place green beans in a bowl
3. Mix together remaining ingredients, add green beans and fully coat
4. Place in the air fryer and cook for 12 minutes

Crispy Broccoli

Servings: 2
Cooking Time:xx

Ingredients:

- 170 g/6 oz. broccoli florets
- 2 tablespoons olive oil
- ⅛ teaspoon garlic salt
- ⅛ teaspoon freshly ground black pepper
- 2 tablespoons freshly grated Parmesan or Pecorino

Directions:

1. Preheat the air-fryer to 200°C/400°F.
2. Toss the broccoli in the oil, season with the garlic salt and pepper, then toss over the grated cheese and combine well. Add the broccoli to the preheated air-fryer and air-fry for 5 minutes, giving the broccoli a stir halfway through to ensure even cooking.

Butternut Squash

Servings: 4
Cooking Time:xx

Ingredients:

- 500 g/1 lb. 2 oz. butternut squash, chopped into 2.5-cm/1-in. cubes
- 1 tablespoon olive oil or avocado oil
- 1 teaspoon smoked paprika
- 1 teaspoon dried oregano
- ½ teaspoon salt
- ¼ teaspoon freshly ground black pepper

Directions:

1. Preheat the air-fryer to 180ºC/350ºF.
2. In a bowl toss the butternut squash cubes in the oil and all the seasonings.
3. Add the butternut squash cubes to the preheated air-fryer and air-fry for 16–18 minutes, shaking the drawer once during cooking.

Crispy Cinnamon French Toast

Servings:2
Cooking Time:5 Minutes

Ingredients:

- 4 slices white bread
- 4 eggs
- 200 ml milk (cow's milk, cashew milk, soy milk, or oat milk)
- 2 tbsp granulated sugar
- 1 tsp brown sugar
- 1 tsp vanilla extract
- ½ tsp ground cinnamon

Directions:

1. Preheat your air fryer to 150 °C / 300 °F and line the bottom of the basket with parchment paper.
2. Cut each of the bread slices into 2 even rectangles and set them aside.
3. In a mixing bowl, whisk together the 4 eggs, milk, granulated sugar, brown sugar, vanilla extract, and ground cinnamon.
4. Soak the bread pieces in the egg mixture until they are fully covered and soaked in the mixture.
5. Place the coated bread slices in the lined air fryer, close the lid, and cook for 4-5 minutes until the bread is crispy and golden.
6. Serve the French toast slices with whatever toppings you desire.

Ricotta Stuffed Aubergine

Servings: 2
Cooking Time:xx

Ingredients:

- 1 aubergine
- 150g ricotta cheese
- 75g Parmesan cheese, plus an extra 75g for the breading
- 1 tsp garlic powder
- 3 tbsp parsley
- 1 egg, plus an extra 2 eggs for the breading
- 300g pork rind crumbs
- 2 tsp Italian seasoning

Directions:

1. Cut the aubergine into rounds, about 1/2" in thickness
2. Line a baking sheet with parchment and arrange the rounds on top, sprinkling with salt
3. Place another sheet of parchment on top and place something heavy on top to get rid of excess water
4. Leave for 30 minutes
5. Take a bowl and combine the egg, ricotta, 75g Parmesan and parsley, until smooth
6. Remove the parchment from the aubergine and wipe off the salt
7. Take a tablespoon of the ricotta mixture and place on top of each round of aubergine, spreading with a knife
8. Place in the freezer for a while to set
9. Take a bowl and add the two eggs, the pork rinds, parmesan and seasonings, and combine
10. Remove the aubergine from the freezer and coat each one in the mixture completely
11. Place back in the freezer for 45 minutes
12. Cook in the air fryer for 8 minutes at 250°C

Carrot & Parmesan Chips

Servings: 2
Cooking Time:xx

Ingredients:

- 180g carrots
- 1 tbsp olive oil
- 2 tbsp grated parmesan
- 1 crushed garlic clove
- Salt and pepper for seasoning

Directions:

1. Take a mixing bowl and add the olive oil and garlic, combining well
2. Remove the tops of the carrots and cut into halves, and then another half
3. Add the carrots to the bowl and toss well
4. Add the parmesan and coat the carrots well
5. Add the carrots to the air fryer and cook for 20 minutes at 220°C, shaking halfway through

Crispy Sweet & Spicy Cauliflower

Servings: 2
Cooking Time:xx

Ingredients:

- ½ a head of cauliflower
- 1 teaspoon sriracha sauce
- 1 teaspoon soy sauce (or tamari)
- ½ teaspoon maple syrup
- 2 teaspoons olive oil or avocado oil

Directions:

1. Preheat the air-fryer to 180ºC/350ºF.
2. Chop the cauliflower into florets with a head size of roughly 5 cm/1 in. Place the other ingredients in a bowl and mix together, then add the florets and toss to coat them.
3. Add the cauliflower to the preheated air-fryer and air-fry for 12 minutes, shaking the drawer a couple of times during cooking.

Air Fryer Corn On The Cob

Servings: 2
Cooking Time:xx

Ingredients:

- 2 corn on the cob
- 2 tbsp melted butter
- A pinch of salt
- 1/2 tsp dried parsley
- 2 tbsp grated parmesan

Directions:

1. Preheat the air fryer to 270ºC
2. Take a bowl and combine the melted butter, salt and parsley
3. Brush the corn with the mixture
4. Add the corn inside the air fryer and cook for 14 minutes
5. Remove the corn from the fryer and roll in the grated cheese

Sweet And Sticky Parsnips And Carrots

Servings:2
Cooking Time:15 Minutes

Ingredients:

- 4 large carrots, peeled and chopped into long chunks
- 4 large parsnips, peeled and chopped into long chunks
- 1 tbsp olive oil
- 2 tbsp honey
- 1 tsp dried mixed herbs

Directions:

1. Preheat the air fryer to 150 °C / 300 °F and line the bottom of the basket with parchment paper.
2. Place the chopped carrots and parsnips in a large bowl and drizzle over the olive oil and honey. Sprinkle in some black pepper to taste and toss well to fully coat the vegetables.
3. Transfer the coated vegetables into the air fryer basket and shut the lid. Cook for 20 minutes until the carrots and parsnips and cooked and crispy.
4. Serve as a side with your dinner.

Mediterranean Vegetables

Servings: 1–2
Cooking Time:xx

Ingredients:

- 1 courgette/zucchini, thickly sliced
- 1 (bell) pepper, deseeded and chopped into large chunks
- 1 red onion, sliced into wedges
- 12 cherry tomatoes
- 1 tablespoon olive oil
- ½ teaspoon salt
- ½ teaspoon freshly ground black pepper
- 2 rosemary twigs
- mozzarella, fresh pesto (see page 80) and basil leaves, to serve

Directions:

1. Preheat the air-fryer to 180ºC/350ºF.
2. Toss the prepared vegetables in the oil and seasoning. Add the vegetables and the rosemary to the preheated air-fryer and air-fry for 12–14 minutes, depending on how 'chargrilled' you like them.
3. Remove and serve topped with fresh mozzarella and pesto and scattered with basil leaves.

Courgette Chips

Servings: 4
Cooking Time:xx

Ingredients:

- 250g panko bread crumbs
- 100g grated parmesan
- 1 medium courgette, thinly sliced
- 1 egg beaten

Directions:

1. Preheat the air fryer to 175ºC
2. Combine the breadcrumbs and parmesan
3. Dip the courgette into the egg then coat in bread crumbs
4. Spray with cooking spray and cook in the air fryer for 10 minutes
5. Turnover with tongs and cook for a further 2 minutes

Super Easy Fries

Servings: 2
Cooking Time:xx

Ingredients:

- 500g potatoes cut into ½ inch sticks
- 1 tsp olive oil
- ¼ tsp salt
- ¼ tsp pepper

Directions:

1. Place the potatoes in a bowl cover with water and allow to soak for 30 minutes
2. Spread the butter onto one side of the bread slices
3. Pat dry with paper, drizzle with oil and toss to coat
4. Place in the air fryer and cook at 200ºC for about 15 minutes, keep tossing through cooking time
5. Sprinkle with salt and pepper

Asparagus Fries

Servings: 2
Cooking Time:xx

Ingredients:

- 1 egg
- 1 tsp honey
- 100g panko bread crumbs
- Pinch of cayenne pepper
- 100g grated parmesan
- 12 asparagus spears
- 75g mustard
- 75g Greek yogurt

Directions:

1. Preheat air fryer to 200ºC
2. Combine egg and honey in a bowl, mix panko crumbs and parmesan on a plate
3. Coat each asparagus in egg then in the bread crumbs
4. Place in the air fryer and cook for about 6 mins
5. Mix the remaining ingredients in a bowl and serve as a dipping sauce

Orange Sesame Cauliflower

Servings: 4
Cooking Time:xx

Ingredients:

- 100ml water
- 30g cornstarch
- 50g flour
- 1/2 tsp salt
- ½ tsp pepper
- 2 tbsp tomato ketchup
- 2 tbsp brown sugar
- 1 sliced onion

Directions:

1. Mix together flour, cornstarch, water, salt and pepper until smooth
2. Coat the cauliflower and chill for 30 minutes
3. Place in the air fryer and cook for 22 minutes at 170ºC
4. Meanwhile combine remaining ingredients in a saucepan, gently simmer until thickened.
5. Mix cauliflower with sauce and top with toasted sesame seeds to serve

Roasted Okra

Servings: 1
Cooking Time:xx

Ingredients:

- 300g Okra, ends trimmed and pods sliced
- 1 tsp olive oil
- ¼ tsp salt
- ⅛ tsp pepper

Directions:

1. Preheat the air fryer to 175ºC
2. Combine all ingredients in a bowl and stir gently
3. Place in the air fryer and cook for 5 minutes, shake and cook for another 5 minutes

Honey Roasted Parsnips

Servings: 4
Cooking Time:xx

Ingredients:

- 350 g/12 oz. parsnips
- 1 tablespoon plain/all-purpose flour (gluten-free if you wish)
- 1½ tablespoons runny honey
- 2 tablespoons olive oil
- salt

Directions:

1. Top and tail the parsnips, then slice lengthways, about 2 cm/¾ in. wide. Place in a saucepan with water to cover and a good pinch of salt. Bring to the boil, then boil for 5 minutes.
2. Remove and drain well, allowing any excess water to evaporate. Dust the parsnips with flour. Mix together the honey and oil in a small bowl, then toss in the parsnips to coat well in the honey and oil.
3. Preheat the air-fryer to 180ºC/350ºF.
4. Add the parsnips to the preheated air-fryer and air-fry for 14–16 minutes, depending on how dark you like the outsides (the longer you cook them, the sweeter they get).

Desserts Recipes

Lemon Buns

Servings: 12
Cooking Time:xx
Ingredients:

- 100g butter
- 100g caster sugar
- 2 eggs
- 100g self raising flour
- ½ tsp vanilla essence
- 1 tsp cherries
- 50g butter
- 100g icing sugar
- ½ small lemon rind and juice

Directions:

1. Preheat the air fryer to 170ºC
2. Cream the 100g butter, sugar and vanilla together until light and fluffy
3. Beat in the eggs one at a time adding a little flour with each
4. Fold in the remaining flour
5. Half fill bun cases with the mix, place in the air fryer and cook for 8 minutes
6. Cream 50g butter then mix in the icing sugar, stir in the lemon
7. Slice the top off each bun and create a butterfly shape using the icing to hold together. Add a 1/3 cherry to each one

Fruit Scones

Servings: 4
Cooking Time:xx
Ingredients:

- 225g self raising flour
- 50g butter
- 50g sultanas
- 25g caster sugar
- 1 egg
- A little milk

Directions:

1. Place the flour in a bowl and rub in the butter, add the sultanas and mix
2. Stir in the caster sugar
3. Add the egg and mix well
4. Add a little bit of milk at a time to form a dough
5. Shape the dough into scones
6. Place in the air fryer and bake at 180ºC for 8 minutes

Apple Pie

Servings: 2
Cooking Time:xx

Ingredients:

- 1 packet of ready made pastry
- 1 apple, chopped
- 2 tsp lemon juice
- 1 tsp cinnamon
- 2 tbsp sugar
- ½ tsp vanilla extract
- 1 tbsp butter
- 1 beaten egg
- 1 tbsp raw sugar

Directions:

1. Preheat the air fryer to 160ºC
2. Line a baking tin with pastry
3. Mix the apple, lemon juice, cinnamon, sugar and vanilla in a bowl
4. Pour the apple mix into the tin with the pastry, top with chunks of butter
5. Cover with a second piece of pastry, place three slits in the top of the pastry
6. Brush the pastry with beaten egg and sprinkle with raw sugar
7. Place in the air fryer and cook for 30 minutes

Thai Style Bananas

Servings: 4
Cooking Time:xx

Ingredients:

- 4 ripe bananas
- 2 tbsp flour
- 2 tbsp rice flour
- 2 tbsp corn flour
- 2 tbsp desiccated coconut
- Pinch salt
- ½ tsp baking powder
- Sesame seeds

Directions:

1. Add all the ingredients to a bowl apart from the sesame seeds mix well
2. Line the air fryer with foil
3. Dip the banana into the batter mix then roll in the sesame seeds
4. Place in the air fryer and cook for about 15 minutes at 200ºC turning halfway

Chocolate-glazed Banana Slices

Servings:2
Cooking Time:10 Minutes

Ingredients:

- 2 bananas
- 1 tbsp honey
- 1 tbsp chocolate spread, melted
- 2 tbsp milk chocolate chips

Directions:

1. Preheat the air fryer to 180 °C / 350 °F. Remove the mesh basket from the machine and line it with parchment paper.
2. Cut the two bananas into even slices and place them in the lined air fryer basket.
3. In a small bowl, mix the honey and melted chocolate spread. Use a brush to glaze the banana slices. Carefully press the milk chocolate chips into the banana slices enough so that they won't fall out when you transfer the bananas into the air fryer.
4. Carefully slide the mesh basket into the air fryer, close the lid, and cook for 10 minutes until the bananas are hot and the choc chips have melted.
5. Enjoy the banana slices on their own or with a side of ice cream.

Lava Cakes

Servings: 4
Cooking Time:xx

Ingredients:

- 1 ½ tbsp self raising flour
- 3 ½ tbsp sugar
- 150g butter
- 150g dark chocolate, chopped
- 2 eggs

Directions:

1. Preheat the air fryer to 175ºC
2. Grease 4 ramekin dishes
3. Melt chocolate and butter in the microwave for about 3 minutes
4. Whisk the eggs and sugar together until pale and frothy
5. Pour melted chocolate into the eggs and stir in the flour
6. Fill the ramekins ¾ full, place in the air fryer and cook for 10 minutes

Special Oreos

Servings: 9
Cooking Time:xx

Ingredients:

- 100g pancake mix
- 25ml water
- Cooking spray
- 9 Oreos
- 1 tbsp icing sugar

Directions:

1. Mix pancake mix and water until well combined
2. Line the air fryer with parchment paper and spray with cooking spray
3. Preheat the air fryer to 200ºC
4. Dip each cookie in the pancake mix and place in the air fryer
5. Cook for 5 minutes, turn and cook for a further 3 minutes
6. Sprinkle with icing sugar to serve

Zebra Cake

Servings: 6
Cooking Time:xx
Ingredients:

- 115g butter
- 2 eggs
- 100g caster sugar
- 1 tbsp cocoa powder
- 100g self raising flour
- 30ml milk
- 1tsp vanilla

Directions:

1. Preheat air fryer to 160ºC
2. Line a 6 inch baking tin
3. Beat together the butter and sugar until light and fluffy
4. Add eggs one at a time then add the vanilla and milk
5. Add the flour and mix well
6. Divide the mix in half
7. Add cocoa powder to half the mix and mix well
8. Add a scoop of each of the batters at a time until it's all in the tin, place in the air fryer and cook for 30 minutes

Peanut Butter & Chocolate Baked Oats

Servings:9
Cooking Time:xx
Ingredients:

- 150 g/1 heaped cup rolled oats/quick-cooking oats
- 50 g/⅓ cup dark chocolate chips or buttons
- 300 ml/1¼ cups milk or plant-based milk
- 50 g/3½ tablespoons Greek or plant-based yogurt
- 1 tablespoon runny honey or maple syrup
- ½ teaspoon ground cinnamon or ground ginger
- 65 g/scant ⅓ cup smooth peanut butter

Directions:

1. Stir all the ingredients together in a bowl, then transfer to a baking dish that fits your air-fryer drawer.
2. Preheat the air-fryer to 180ºC/350ºF.
3. Add the baking dish to the preheated air-fryer and air-fry for 10 minutes. Remove from the air-fryer and serve hot, cut into 9 squares.

Brazilian Pineapple

Servings: 2
Cooking Time:xx
Ingredients:

- 1 small pineapple, cut into spears
- 100g brown sugar
- 2 tsp cinnamon
- 3 tbsp melted butter

Directions:

1. Mix the brown sugar and cinnamon together in a small bowl
2. Brush the pineapple with melted butter
3. Sprinkle with the sugar and cinnamon
4. Heat the air fryer to 200ºC
5. Cook the pineapple for about 10 minutes

Apple Fritters

Servings: 4
Cooking Time:xx

Ingredients:

- 225g self raising flour
- 200g greek yogurt
- 2 tsp sugar
- 1 tbsp cinnamon
- 1 apple peeled and chopped
- 225g icing sugar
- 2 tbsp milk

Directions:

1. Mix the flour, yogurt, sugar, cinnamon and apple together. Knead for about 3 -4 minutes
2. Mix the icing sugar and milk together to make the glaze and set aside
3. Line the air fryer with parchment paper and spray with cooking spray
4. Divide the fritter mix into four, flatten each portion and place in the air fryer
5. Cook at 185ºC for about 15 minutes turning halfway
6. Drizzle with glaze to serve

French Toast Sticks

Servings: 12
Cooking Time:xx

Ingredients:

- 2 eggs
- 25g milk
- 1 tbsp melted butter
- 1 tsp vanilla extract
- 1 tsp cinnamon
- 4 slices bread, cut into thirds
- 1 tsp icing sugar

Directions:

1. Mix eggs, milk, butter, vanilla and cinnamon together in a bowl
2. Line the air fryer with parchment paper
3. Dip each piece of bread into the egg mixture
4. Place in the air fryer and cook at 190ºC for 6 minutes, turn over and cook for another 3 minutes
5. Sprinkle with icing sugar to serve

Apple Chips With Yogurt Dip

Servings: 4
Cooking Time:xx

Ingredients:

- 1 apple
- 1 tsp cinnamon
- 2 tsp oil
- Cooking spray
- 25g greek yogurt
- 1 tbsp almond butter
- 1 tsp honey

Directions:

1. Thinly slice the apple, place in a bowl and coat with cinnamon and oil
2. Coat the air fryer with cooking spray and add the apple slices
3. Cook the slices for 12 minutes at 180ºC
4. Mix the butter, honey and yogurt together and serve with the apple slices as a dip

Peach Pies

Servings: 8
Cooking Time:xx

Ingredients:

- 2 peaches, peeled and chopped
- 1 tbsp lemon juice
- 3 tbsp sugar
- 1 tsp vanilla extract
- ¼ tsp salt
- 1 tsp cornstarch
- 1 pack of shortcrust pastry

Directions:

1. Stir together peaches, lemon juice, sugar, vanilla and salt allow to stand for 15 minutes
2. Drain the peaches keeping 1 tbsp of the juice
3. Mix the liquid with the cornstarch and mix into the peaches
4. Cut out 8 4 inch circles from the pastry. Add 1 tbsp of peach mix to each piece of pastry
5. Fold the dough over to create half moons, crimp the edges with a fork to seal. Spray with cooking spray
6. Place in the air fryer and cook at 180°C for 12-14 minutes

Cherry Pies

Servings: 6
Cooking Time:xx

Ingredients:

- 300g prepared shortcrust pastry
- 75g cherry pie filling
- Cooking spray
- 3 tbsp icing sugar
- ½ tsp milk

Directions:

1. Cut out 6 pies with a cookie cutter
2. Add 1 ½ tbsp filling to each pie
3. Fold the dough in half and seal around the edges with a fork
4. Place in the air fryer, spray with cooking spray
5. Cook at 175°C for 10 minutes
6. Mix icing sugar and milk and drizzled over cooled pies to serve

Apple Crumble

Servings: 4
Cooking Time:xx

Ingredients:

- 2 apples (each roughly 175 g/6 oz.), cored and chopped into 2-cm/¾-in cubes
- 3 tablespoons unrefined sugar
- 100 g/1 cup jumbo rolled oats/old-fashioned oats
- 40 g/heaped ¼ cup flour (gluten-free if you wish)
- 1 heaped teaspoon ground cinnamon
- 70 g/scant ⅓ cup cold butter, chopped into small cubes

Directions:

1. Preheat the air-fryer to 180ºC/350ºF.
2. Scatter the apple pieces in a baking dish that fits your air-fryer, then sprinkle over 1 tablespoon sugar. Add the baking dish to the preheated air-fryer and air-fry for 5 minutes.
3. Meanwhile, in a bowl mix together the oats, flour, remaining sugar and cold butter. Use your fingertips to bring the crumble topping together.
4. Remove the baking dish from the air-fryer and spoon the crumble topping over the partially cooked apple. Return the baking dish to the air dryer and air-fry for a further 10 minutes. Serve warm or cold.

Chonut Holes

Servings: 12
Cooking Time:xx

Ingredients:

- 225g flour
- 75g sugar
- 1 tsp baking powder
- ¼ tsp cinnamon
- 2 tbsp sugar
- ½ tsp salt
- 2 tbsp aquafaba
- 1 tbsp melted coconut oil
- 75ml soy milk
- 2 tsp cinnamon

Directions:

1. In a bowl mix the flour, ¼ cup sugar, baking powder, ¼ tsp cinnamon and salt
2. Add the aquafaba, coconut oil and soy milk mix well
3. In another bowl mix 2 tsp cinnamon and 2 tbsp sugar
4. Line the air fryer with parchment paper
5. Divide the dough into 12 pieces and dredge with the cinnamon sugar mix
6. Place in the air fryer at 185ºC and cook for 6-8 minutes, don't shake them

Birthday Cheesecake

Servings: 8
Cooking Time:xx

Ingredients:

- 6 Digestive biscuits
- 50g melted butter
- 800g soft cheese
- 500g caster sugar
- 4 tbsp cocoa powder
- 6 eggs
- 2 tbsp honey
- 1 tbsp vanilla

Directions:

1. Flour a spring form tin to prevent sticking
2. Crush the biscuits and then mix with the melted butter, press into the bottom and sides of the tin
3. Mix the caster sugar and soft cheese with an electric mixer. Add 5 eggs, honey and vanilla. Mix well
4. Spoon half the mix into the pan and pat down well. Place in the air fryer and cook at 180ºC for 20 minutes then 160ºC for 15 minutes and then 150ºC for 20 minutes
5. Mix the cocoa and the last egg into the remaining mix. Spoon over the over the bottom layer and place in the fridge. Chill for 11 hours

Thai Fried Bananas

Servings: 8
Cooking Time:xx

Ingredients:

- 4 ripe bananas
- 2 tbsp flour
- 2 tbsp rice flour
- 2 tbsp cornflour
- 2 tbsp desiccated coconut
- Pinch salt
- ½ tsp baking powder
- ½ tsp cardamon powder

Directions:

1. Place all the dry ingredients in a bowl and mix well. Add a little water at a time and combine to form a batter
2. Cut the bananas in half and then half again length wise
3. Line the air fryer with parchment paper and spray with cooking spray
4. Dip each banana piece in the batter mix and place in the air fryer
5. Cook at 200ºC for 10 -15 minutes turning halfway
6. Serve with ice cream

Banana And Nutella Sandwich

Servings: 2
Cooking Time:xx

Ingredients:

- Softened butter
- 4 slices white bread
- 25g chocolate spread
- 1 banana

Directions:

1. Preheat the air fryer to 185ºC
2. Spread butter on one side of all the bread slices
3. Spread chocolate spread on the other side of each slice
4. Add sliced banana to two slices of bread then add the other slice of bread to each
5. Cut in half diagonally to form triangles
6. Place in the air fryer and cook for 5 minutes turn over and cook for another 2 minutes

Appendix : Recipes Index

A

B

C

E

F

G

H

T

V

W

Z

Printed in Great Britain
by Amazon

26046108R10051